59 Recruiting Secrets
for Retailers

59 Recruiting Secrets for Retailers

*How to Find and Attract Great
Prospective Associates For Your Store*

James W. Cole

authorHOUSE®

AuthorHouse™
1663 Liberty Drive
Bloomington, IN 47403
www.authorhouse.com
Phone: 1-800-839-8640

First published by AuthorHouse   06/17/2011

ISBN: 978-1-4634-0795-7 (sc)
ISBN: 978-1-4634-0794-0 (ebk)

Library of Congress Control Number: 2011908582

Printed in the United States of America

Any people depicted in stock imagery provided by Thinkstock are models, and such images are being used for illustrative purposes only.
Certain stock imagery © Thinkstock.

This book is printed on acid-free paper.

Dedication

To my family

Diane,
my wife,
patient and constantly supportive.

Samantha & Dan
and
Mike & Stephenie,
my children and their spouses,
my motivation.

Hailey, Ashley, Katie, and William,
my grandchildren,
my inspiration.

THANK YOU!

The SECRET Contents

A Problem Of Perception

In late March of 2011 I heard something profound on the radio. A well-known retail "expert" was being interviewed by a local, morning talk show host.

The "expert" said:

"If you are a small business owner and WalMart comes to your town, you should just give up . . ."

As I continued to listen to the interview, I realized that there was nothing sarcastic or tongue-in-cheek about the remark.

The "expert" was serious!

He honestly believed that, in the face of a withering WalMart attack (a super store, or one of the smaller versions, moving into your town), you (a small/medium-sized, local retailer) should just close your doors and apply to be a greeter—"Welcome to WalMart!" (I hope that isn't copyrighted!)

I know people who would have been outraged and offended, or inconsolably saddened, by this assertion. I, on the other hand, was amazed and impressed.

This is exactly the message that I would expect WalMart and the big box, mega stores to be spreading:

"GIVE UP! You can't compete against us. We're too big! We're too good! We have everything that the public needs and wants. You are too small and you don't have a chance!"

Their message is compelling and logical. They have everything working to their benefit—price, selection, location, advertising! The little guys can't win!

At least that is what they want you to think.

Over the years this form of competition has been referred to as "trash talk" or "smack." In our society, it is a highly effective and perfectly acceptable method of psyching out a competitor.

When I was younger and playing baseball, the players on the other team would say, *"He can't hit it! He can't hit it! Swing, Batter, Swing!"* I would like to tell you that I was too smart to fall for that tactic, but I wasn't and I normally swung away to the laughter of my "mean, heartless" competition.

Today, kids playing sports have been taught that competition is bad. Everyone is a winner and no one is a loser.

Sorry, but that isn't the way it works in the real World.

In the big game of life, there are winners and losers. And there are business owners who buy the hype that some winners can't be beaten. When the mean, old industry giants show up, they are ready to follow the "expert's" advice, fold their tents and go home.

This is simply a problem of perception!

Too few retailers recognize the trash talk for what it is—a carefully crafted fabrication—a bald-faced LIE!

It was created by the giants to crush the spirits of the smaller stores and keep attention away from their Achilles Heel.

Yes, that's right the biggies have a weakness!

This is no longer about WalMart alone. <u>All</u> of the giants suffer from the same fatal short-coming.

No matter what the venerable, highly-respected news-anchor may say, or what the flashy commercials may tout, the big-box, mega stores (and the Internet, for that matter) lack SERVICE.

How do you keep a secret that is so obviously NOT A SECRET?

The answer is simple—You make a lot of noise!

Noise about what you <u>do</u> have (low, low prices, for example) and even more noise about what your competition doesn't have (any chance of beating you, for example) and no one will notice your biggest secret (lousy service, for example)!

A FUNNY THING ABOUT SECRETS

This book is all about SECRETS!

Not just the secret weakness disclosed above, but also secrets about how to take advantage of that short-coming!

We are going to talk about secrets that can:

- increase sales,
- improve team morale
- increase customer satisfaction and loyalty
- solve the problem of mega store mind-games once and for all

A funny thing about these secrets: They tend to be the really GREAT ideas!

When was the last time you heard of a really bad business idea that had been kept secret for years?

No one hides bad techniques, bad ideas or bad concepts. They aren't secrets. They are "common knowledge." They are displayed clearly for everyone to see. Everyone knows about them and a lot of managers use them regularly because they are well known, widely accepted and easy to implement.

So why are so many great business practices so secret? Here are four possible answers:

<u>First</u>, they might just be common sense concepts which have been overlooked or ignored in the hustle and bustle of everyday business life.

<u>Second</u>, they may have been hidden intentionally in order to preserve personal power or market dominance (Who would do something like that?).

<u>Third</u>, the secret holders may feel that they have no incentive to disclose the secret(s) ("What do I get out of it?").

And finally, <u>fourth</u>, it may be due to laziness. Great business ideas sometimes require planning and effort. (Don't worry! None of the secrets in this book require <u>any</u> planning or effort. I also know how you can lose 100 pounds in a week—without drugs, workouts or changing the way you eat!)

Regardless of the motivation for keeping them, great business secrets can often be revealed by close observation.

The problem is that most of us don't have the time (or the patience) to watch successful managers until all of their secrets are disclosed.

That's where this book comes into play. Throughout my thirty year sales career I have had the opportunity to watch and work with some of the best managers and salespeople in the Country. They haven't always been the smartest, the most naturally talented, the most politically astute or the most attractive. They were and are driven, perceptive and persistent. They are champions in every sense of the word. I have simply compiled some of their best strategies (secrets) in the pages that follow.

Let's begin with perhaps the most important secret of them all.

SECRET #1—GOOD SERVICE IS THE PRODUCT OF GOOD PEOPLE!

". . . but with service like that, I don't care how much it costs!"

Quote from satisfied customer—
TV commercial for angieslist.com

According to today's mega store/Internet retail paradigm (way of thinking), customers enter and return to a "store" for <u>only</u> four possible reasons:

- **L**ocation, location, location;
- **A**dvertising
- **P**roduct selection
- **P**rice

If you buy into this thought process (we will call it—LAPP), store employees are no longer a real factor in business success. Associates—their attitudes, appearance and behavior—are far less important than giant selections, flashy ads, wide aisles, one-click convenience and low, low, low everyday prices.

Of course, this way of thinking makes it almost impossible for small/medium-sized retailers to compete head-to-head and toe-to-toe with the "Big Guys." As we discussed earlier, when the news leaks out that a retail giant is coming to town many store owners will simply hang their heads and give up without a fight. I am sure that <u>none</u> of the mega stores or big boxes intend for this to happen (tongue planted firmly in cheek).

And yet . . .

The reality is that in spite of the "convenience," low prices and incredible selections at the mega stores or on the Internet, customers still go to some of the poorly advertised local retailers who are inconvenient, have less selection with higher prices, and haven't opted to go out of business.

With all the hype about retail ghost towns, created by LAPP retailers, even some tiny stores still flourish.

Why?

There are only two possible answers—

Unique, exclusive, product selections and

People (associates, specifically sales associates)

While it is certainly possible for a small, local retailer to offer unique products or designer brands which are not available in the big box stores, it is <u>impossible</u> for the local store to sell products which are not available on the Internet. So, "unique, exclusive product selection" can't be the answer.

That leaves PEOPLE!

Even if you are a complete sellout to the LAPP mindset, you will immediately recognize the truth of the following statement.

CUSTOMERS NEED HELP.

Regardless of the location, the products, the selection or the price—customers need help.

They have questions.

They have concerns.

They have complaints.

They have special needs.

Another word for "help" is service.

CUSTOMERS NEED **SERVICE**!

SERVICE <u>REQUIRES</u> HELPFUL EMPLOYEES!

Okay, let's take a moment and test our LAPP thought process.

Do customers <u>need</u> location, advertising, product selection or low prices in order to purchase retail goods?

My answer would be, "NO," in capital letters, emphatically, no doubt, without question!

Customers <u>want</u> location, advertising, product selection and low prices, but they don't <u>need</u> them. LAPP is nice, but it isn't necessary. What is necessary?

HELP! Service!

The big box, Internet, LAPP retailers have a perfect answer to the problem—give customers an "800/888" number (a direct connection to a foreign country) or force the "valued" customers to track down a "warm, friendly" (according to their advertisements) associate (who generally has no idea where the super glue or the brown rice is located).

Oh, sorry, I almost forgot about the long lines you can stand in at the "Customer Service" counter. You know what I am talking about. You and twenty of your closest strangers waiting to talk to ONE friendly, out-going customer service "specialist." Sounds like the Post Office, doesn't it?

In the minds of the "Big Boys" this level of service is "good enough."

The Mega store says, *"This is 'good enough' works because we have the lowest prices in town!"*

Internet retailer says, *"'Good enough' works because it keeps our costs down and allows us to offer the lowest prices on the Net!"*

And yet . . .

Customers <u>still</u> go to the local, small/medium-sized retailer who is out of the way and charges more, but who can and does provide some real service.

The most important secret of them all has two parts.

First, GOOD service <u>sells</u>—not occasional service, not some service, not lip service—GOOD service!

The quote at the top of the page is true. Very often, customers will forego the "lowest price in town" <u>and</u> the "lowest price on the Net" in order to be treated fairly and have their concerns dealt with quickly.

Second, in <u>every</u> case, the good service they seek is the product of high-quality, friendly, helpful associates.

Simple? Yes. Logical? Yes.

And yet . . .

Those same small/medium retailers recruit and hire some amazingly bad people to provide the only product which separates them from the big box/internet competitors: SERVICE!

When asked, most of those store owners or managers will say that they hired the best people available.

This just isn't true!

Great employees are out there. You just have to know where and how to look for them.

And how does a manager know how and where to look for great employees?

Until now, it was a secret! Read on.

Secret #2—Everyone Sells!

Some retailers still have a business paradigm that belongs in a prior century—

"I don't have 'sales associates' in my store. My employees are 'clerks,' 'counter-help,' 'hourly checkers,' 'office staff,' 'delivery drivers,' 'customer service representatives' or just plain 'associates.'"

Here is a "secret" attitude that leads to success:

<u>Every</u> retail associate is in sales, whether they realize it or not. They sell every customer with whom they come into contact on returning to shop in the store, or on <u>not</u> returning to shop in the store <u>ever</u>!

They make their sales presentation by their appearance, their attitude, their performance and even their <u>smell</u>.

If the person at the register is smiling and pleasant, the customer is more likely to enjoy their shopping experience and consider returning. If the checker is inattentive and busy talking with co-workers, or even worse, talking on a cell phone, the customer will probably leave and never come back. Believe me, either way, the customer has been SOLD!

Similarly, even if other parts of the shopping experience were pleasant, a surly, smelly delivery truck driver can turn a customer off (<u>off</u> of <u>ever</u> shopping in the store again).

If driver is pleasant, clean and efficient, he/she can be a positive influence on a possible return shopping trip.

This secret applies to the manager/owner, the office/administrative staff, the people on the floor <u>and</u> the warehouse/delivery crew—<u>everyone</u> in the store who is seen by, or speaks to, a customer.

Some retailers actually believe, naively, that their products sell themselves!

This is a subversive, destructive lesson which was probably learned from the big box/internet retailers. Now don't get me wrong, some products do sell themselves, but not every store wants to sell super glue or brown rice (By the way, where are they located?).

The mega stores and the web have painted themselves into a corner. If their products don't sell themselves, they aren't going to sell at all because there is no real help or service available.

It just can't work that way in smaller stores, if they want to stay in business.

So, which will it be—the positive, "come back soon" sales approach, or the negative, "we don't care about your business" sales presentation? You decide, in part, by the candidates who you recruit to work in your store.

Recruiting great prospective associates can make retail life much more enjoyable and profitable. Recognizing the fact that you are looking for <u>excellent</u> sales people, not "good" or "okay" sales people, is a sign of management maturity.

Start recruiting <u>great</u> candidates right away! Don't accept anyone less!

Secret #3—Take Action!
Repeat Daily!

For some odd reason, a weird habit has been instilled within us.

We have been taught that we should read an entire how-to book before we start implementing any of the ideas it contains.

Our elementary teachers probably said something like this, "You might get things out of order!"

Not so with this book!

One great secret to success is: Don't hesitate! Don't procrastinate! Don't wait to get started!

TAKE ACTION!!

Remember, greatness grows from action, not deliberation!

Choose a secret—any secret—and implement it immediately. Yes, you may even read ahead in the book. You have my permission.

The secret techniques contained herein are in no particular order and most of them aren't dependent on the others to work properly.

Make it a habit to try at least one new secret _everyday_!!

By working this way, you will begin to make needed CHANGE painlessly! Yes, there it is, I said it! "Change" has been introduced to our discussion.

It can be scary, I know, but believe me, you'll get used to it, and the results will pay BIG dividends!

Secret #4—Where You Fish Matters!

Take a moment and try this simple test:

Walk into a retail store—anytime, anywhere (other than your own store, of course).

Any retailer will do; a clothing store, a furniture store, a convenience store or even a café/restaurant (yes, it's a retail store, too—it sells prepared food—with commissioned sales associates).

When you enter the store, it is possible that an enthusiastic, positive, <u>smiling</u>, clean, well-dressed associate will offer a friendly greeting, followed immediately by a sincere offer of service.

It is also possible that an individual will provide correct answers to questions and meaningful support in the purchase process.

As you are leaving the store, the employee might even say "Thank You" and invite you to come back again soon.

Yes, it is possible that all of that might happen, but it isn't <u>probable</u>!

It is more likely that you will not be greeted at all, or you will be asked a negative question like, "Can I help you?" by a surly, disinterested employee who is wearing dirty, mismatched or wrinkled clothes that smell like cigarettes (or worse).

A broad indictment like this is bound to draw some emotional responses. I can hear managers and company officials everywhere yelling, "Not my people!!"

Perhaps this doesn't describe your associates. Perhaps you are just floating peacefully on the river (d'Nile).

Let's be clear. I'm not just a sales trainer/recruiter/manager (and your humble author). I am also a customer.

In the last few years, I have traveled all over the Country. Everywhere I go, retailers are singing the praises of their "smiling, happy, professional" employees who provide "extraordinary" customer service.

The majority of the associates with whom I have dealt do not live up to those high expectations.

In the real world, retail managers and store owners <u>may</u> be working long hours to build quality associate teams, but the outcome simply does not match the propaganda offered by the "powers-that-be."

Talk to store managers (and I have). They will tell you that they can't find "good" people.

Why?

Prevailing thought (Status Quo) says that retail jobs pay too little and no one wants to work the hours or the weekends.

And yet . . .

A few managers have great teams of enthusiastic, happy, effective "sales" associates, many of whom have worked for the same store for YEARS!

If it is so hard to find <u>any</u> good people, why do some stores appear to have nothing but good people?

There are two answers. Here is the secret:

- Success really does breed success! (We will discuss the power of referrals [another secret] later.)

- Most retail managers are (sorry for the weak music reference) "looking for love in all the wrong places!"

Here is a fishing question for you (You don't even have to know <u>anything</u> about fishing to answer correctly! It does, however, require common sense.):

If you were going fishing today, where would you be the most likely to have success?

In this case, "success" is defined as—lots of large, healthy, hungry fish, easily available to catch.

If you are smart (and I bet you are), you probably wouldn't choose to cast your line into a brown, polluted cesspool.

You would probably choose a clear, clean body of water with many of the types of fish you want to catch.

This analogy applies to recruiting new talent for your store.

STOP prospecting (fishing) in cesspools and polluted rivers!

Search (fish) for great associates where the best possible associates hang out!

Relax. I'm going to give you some great ideas of where that might be.

In an extension of our fishing analogy, consider Secret #5.

SECRET #5—CATCH AND RELEASE!

For fans of fishing, the phrase "catch and release" means something. It is an expression of pure love for the sport of fishing (and the pure hatred of cleaning fish).

For retailers, it is an expression of pure logic in recruiting new store talent.

The secret here is:

Curb your desperation to hire someone, <u>anyone</u> to fill an opening on your floor! Prospecting requires patience. The first person (or the second person, or the tenth person) in the door may not be your best option!

BE PICKY!

If you catch an applicant who isn't a <u>great</u> candidate to build your sales team—THROW THEM BACK!

The fact that they breathe and walk upright (mostly) doesn't mean that they need to be coming into contact with your customers. They should match your vision of a "great associate" and they <u>must</u> fit into the culture of your store.

Once again, I can hear the objections now:

"Why are you telling us this? This is common sense! I turn away poor candidates all the time!"

I'm sure that you do, but how "poor" are they, really?

Most of the retail managers I have watched turn away the unbelievably terrible candidates, the totally unemployable candidates. The "poor" candidates actually start to look good after seeing enough really awful prospects.

In moments of panic ("I've <u>got</u> to hire someone, RIGHT AWAY!), the candidates who don't quite fit the template of a great (or even a "good") employee sometimes get hired.

The justifications are always the same—

"He was the best I could find!"

"She isn't <u>that</u> bad! I can train her to be good enough!"

The top retail recruiters don't have justifications!

THEY HAVE STANDARDS!

You should, too.

SECRET #6—TOP MANAGERS QUESTION THE STATUS QUO!

What is this "Status Quo," that I mentioned earlier?

In simple terms, it is the way that we always do everything.

Why do we always do things the same old way?

Well, that's a tough one. Maybe it's because it worked in the past or it still works occasionally. Maybe it's because we've been told to do it that way. Maybe it's a habit or we're just afraid to try anything new.

In all likelihood, we follow the Status Quo because it's the path of least resistance. It requires no thinking, no innovation, no planning and, most importantly, no personal responsibility:

"This is the way 'Everyone' does it! If it doesn't work, it's not my fault!"

In recruiting new retail sales associates, the Status Quo says:

"It didn't work today, yesterday or the day before, but it might work tomorrow! We do it this way because this is the way we always do it!"

The Status Quo is SAFE. It provides a feeling of security, certainty and justification.

Questioning the way things have always been done requires some courage. In fact, you might be laughed at. You might even be called a heretic.

A heretic is a person who opposes or fights the Status Quo.

In the past, heretics were burned at the stake, stoned or hung.

Today, they are shunned as lepers or praised as heroes (not much in between). The good news is that they are no longer abused or killed by angry mobs (most of the time).

Let's summarize.

The status quo is more about security and less about obtaining optimal results.

Here is the big secret—The top retail managers (those who have the great sales teams and enjoy great production) care less about security and more about obtaining best possible outcome. They are heretics! They don't care who laughs at them because they always get the last laugh (all the way to the bank).

Have courage. Be strong. Question the Status Quo!

Just Something to Think About—

What is it called when you do the same thing over and over, expecting different results?

Insanity!

Or . . .

The Status Quo!

SECRET #7—GREAT MANAGERS PRACTICE!

Questioning the Status Quo leads to the c-word, which I mentioned earlier—CHANGE!

Change isn't always pleasant or fun. It may even open us to criticism or ridicule.

And yet . . .

Is there really any other alternative?

Of course there is! Don't change anything! Continue doing what you have always done and you will keep getting the same results you have always gotten! To expect otherwise is INSANITY!

Most retail managers have proven how <u>not</u> to recruit. The results are indisputable! Continuing the Status Quo will continue to produce weak candidates and weak sales (and strong ulcers) over and over again.

If "weak" isn't good enough, change <u>must</u> occur.

The good news is that change <u>doesn't</u> have to be as dangerous as you may have been led to believe.

The key is steady, consistent PRACTICE!

Practice allows you to become comfortable with a new technique and to gradually blend it into everyday use.

The best retail managers and store owners have amazing skills. Those skills didn't just happen over night. They developed over time with <u>regular</u> <u>practice</u>.

The secret is that practice <u>doesn't</u> make you perfect. Practice makes you SUCCESSFUL!

Secret #8—Look For Someone, Not Anyone!

Okay, so who are you looking for?

What does a "perfect" sales associate look like? . . . sound like? . . . act like?

If everyone already knows the answer (and everyone says they do), why is it so hard for most of them to describe the exact characteristics of a Mr. or Ms. Right?

Here is the answer:

The vast majority of store owners and managers have a broad, general, fuzzy, mental image of someone called the "perfect" associate. These managers generally talk about their vision as a "gut feeling" about who is "right" for their store. They use phrases like, *I just know them when I see them.*

The "gut" image is always very flexible. It can vary widely, depending on the day of the week, the number of available prospects, the physical appearance of the applicants and over a million other factors.

Unless they are visited by the Dumb Luck Fairy (Also known as the "I Won the Lottery" Fairy or the "A Super Model Loves Me" Fairy), the majority of retail manager/owners will never see a candidate that could be considered pretty good, much less "perfect."

The scary part is that they are forced to hire weak, "gut hunch" prospects over and over again, because, *"These are the only applications I received and I need someone now!"*

Unlike the fuzzy majority, successful retail managers have very <u>clear</u> goals. They know who they are looking for. They can describe their qualities in great detail and they look for those qualities in every candidate they choose to interview. They consider all of the selection criteria <u>in</u> <u>advance</u> of inviting candidates to talk. Once they have decided who they want, they don't waiver from their vision!

While this may seem simple enough, it is tougher than it appears. The most successful managers are fully prepared to wait until the right prospect is recruited, regardless of how long it takes. They are seldom affected by outside influences or pressures. They know that a hiring mistake could prove more costly than a missed deadline.

In summary, the best are always looking for someone, someone specific, to join their team! Not just anyone will do!

SECRET #9—THEY <u>DON'T</u> RELY ON LUCK!

Luck exists!

It comes in only two flavors—good & bad. If there is no luck at all, it is simply bad luck.

Another word for luck is "chance."

Relying on luck or chance is simply the process of allowing random forces in the universe to create an outcome with little or no input from the victim (you). Rolling the dice or spinning the wheel qualifies as very little input.

Yeah, you guessed it, great retail managers choose not to rely on luck to determine outcomes. They tend to make a significant effort to shape their own destiny.

Of course, luck is always present in one flavor or another, but to rely on it alone tends to be naïve and lazy.

If we consider recruiting specifically, the least successful managers tend to make minimal efforts and hope that a great prospect will walk through their door. The very successful managers tend to make strong, focused efforts to draw as many GREAT prospects as possible and then choose those who meet their expectations. They allow luck to work in their favor, but they don't rely on chance alone.

SECRET #10—THEY DO RELY ON GOALS!

Top retail managers understand, create and consistently use goals in all facets of their business life, including recruiting new associates!

There is no need to get into some big, long lecture about setting goals, but a few important points should be clarified.

GOALS—The Basics

A "dream" is not a goal. It is a wish, a hope, a fuzzy vision of something we would like to see transpire.

A goal, on the other hand, is a clear, concise statement of expectations or destinations.

If a desired outcome does not qualify as a goal, it is a dream. There is no middle ground.

Goals reflect what is important to the goal setter, including values and principles.

A person without goals (also know as a "dreamer") is like a rudderless ship—going nowhere in particular and happy to be going anywhere at all.

Goals help the goal setter to focus and bring energy to bear in the most efficient manner possible.

Goals work best when they a written down. Goals on paper (or on an electronic device) express commitment and make major variances less likely.

Goals lead to the creation of plans. Plans are detailed maps for reaching goals.

SECRET #11 — "PERFECT" JOB CANDIDATES DON'T EXIST!

I know what you are thinking.

Eventually, you are expecting me to say that top retail managers write down all of the characteristics of their "perfect" associate prospect.

Nope.

First, some great managers <u>do</u> write down important characteristics of people they would like to hire, but some don't. They just have them welded into their minds.

I will give you more insight on this later.

Second, none of the greats I have worked with are looking for a "perfect" prospect.

They know "perfect" is an unreasonable expectation. Perfect people don't exist. The best managers are always looking for people who have certain requisite personal qualities and as many desired qualities as possible.

In other words, they are always looking for good or great, not "perfect."

Secret #12—Create A Picture Of Your Great Prospect!

You will find several excellent management secrets contained in this section.

The first, and perhaps the most important, secret is that a "great" prospective employee is defined solely by <u>YOU</u>, the store manager.

You get to determine who <u>you</u> want to work with. Who, in your opinion, would do the best job of serving <u>your</u> customers? Who would fit best within your culture and your team?

Your vision of "greatness" can be molded from a memory of the best employee you have ever had. It could be a person you have met, or someone you have been served by in the past.

Another Secret—Ultimately, your success (or your failure) at recruiting is determined by your ability to create a clear picture of who you want to hire.

One of the simplest ways to develop that picture is to create a list of personal characteristics you are searching for in a new employee.

Here are some possible qualities to consider:

Honest

Goal-oriented, focused, driven
Prompt
Well-Spoken
Intelligent
Happy
Out-Going
Quick (moving and/or thinking)
Attentive
Positive, upbeat
Persistent
Energetic
Enthusiastic
Curious
Competitive
Friendly
Lean
Quick with to smile
Innovative
Tall
Serious
Jovial
Young or Seasoned
Experienced
Fluent in Spanish, French, Swahili, etc.
Employed (versus Unemployed)
Non-smoker
Clean <u>Now</u> (former drugs, crime, etc.)
Attractive
Fragrant (smells good)
Computer/Software Savy
Business Machine Experience (Typing, 10-key, Cash Reg.)
Able to lift 20 pounds

As you can see, on the list, there are some physical traits mentioned along with the personality characteristics.

Here is an important secret to effective, successful prospecting. In order to have a clear picture of a <u>great</u> prospective associate, you must be absolutely honest with yourself. You are selecting the <u>best</u> candidate to serve <u>your</u> customers. NOTHING ELSE MATTERS!

If a candidate exhibits characteristics or physical traits which <u>might</u> have a negative impact on sales, then the prospect is not <u>great</u> and shouldn't be seriously considered, PERIOD.

Let's talk about some specific examples.

If your store has very narrow aisles, or if your store is very large (requiring rapid transitions from one side or end to the other), or if your associates are expected to stand for long periods of time, perhaps an obese or a physically impaired candidate would not be optimal (great).

On the other hand, does it really matter if the prospect is in a wheel chair? It might if the store has stairs or very unreliable elevators.

Could a short person be a "great" job prospect? Of course, unless reaching top shelves is necessary to serve customers.

Do you occasionally need an associate who speaks fluently in another language or would a strong accent turn your customers off? (Yes, this really is a "physical" characteristic?")

I realize that the extreme religion of "political correctness" would like for us to believe that everyone is suitable for every job opening, regardless physical or mental challenges. It's no secret, this just isn't true.

An outstanding sales candidate for your store should be the person <u>you</u> and your customers need them to be. <u>You</u> get to decide!

Secret #13—Stay On Track! Write Down Your List!

Secret—Getting off track is always easier when there is no track to follow!

Get on track and stay on track! Set recruiting goals. The top managers do it!

Great recruiters know that consistency is vital to success. If you get distracted in the process of selecting a candidate, you could easily make a hiring error. Mistakes are generally painful and expensive.

The best way to stay on track during the prospecting (and the interview) process is to write down the list of characteristics that you are looking for in a great employee. Writing the list is preferable to relying on memory. Forgetting an important personal quality could cause a hiring mistake.

It doesn't need to be formal, but the best list is reproducible and available when you are prospecting or conducting an interview. In other words, don't write it on the back of an old envelope or on scratch paper.

Here is an easy way to create your great prospect characteristics list.

First, look at the list above and draw a line through the characteristics that <u>aren't</u> important to you and your customers.

Then add any important characteristics that aren't on the list.

Next, put an **"R"** beside each of the characteristics that are <u>required</u> in every candidate. These are the traits which are non-negotiable. A job prospect will not be hired without <u>all</u> of them.

All of the remaining qualities are your <u>desired</u> characteristics (**"D"**). They aren't required, but they are valuable. They determine if a prospect is great, or merely acceptable.

Acceptable candidates have all of the R's, but only some of the D's. Great candidates have all of the R's and most or all of the D's.

Congratulations! In three steps you have created a solid picture of a <u>great</u> prospect to work in your store. This is a GOAL, not a fuzzy dream. You are looking for prospects who have most, if not all, of your D's.

"How many D's should a candidate be required to have in order to be considered a firm prospect for my store?"

This really is a judgment call, <u>your</u> judgment call. If I were doing the prospecting, I would add one more step. I would go back down my list and put a check mark by my lowest priority D's. These would be the most expendable qualities. If a candidate doesn't have them, they might still be considered, but with reservations.

Here is a rule of thumb. The more desired characteristics a candidate is missing, the bigger training and supervisory "project" he/she will become.

Always ask yourself,

"Will the final result justify the cost (time & money) to get it?"

Secret #14—"You Can't Change The Spots On A Leopard!"

Everyone knows that no manager would intentionally hire a poor candidate to work in their store.

But even the top managers occasionally take a risk and perform a little charity repair work on a "sub-standard" prospect who they like. Don't they?

NO!!

Great managers know (and accept) the fact that "You can't change the spots on a leopard!" Most of them believe that an attempt to change someone's nature or personality is a total waste of time. They have learned this truth the hard way, by trying to perform a human make-over and failing miserably.

This doesn't mean that they won't occasionally work with young or inexperienced prospects who haven't realized their full potential, but they tend to take the risk only when they can feel relatively certain of the outcome.

Secret #15—Their Mission Determines The R's & D's!

Over the years, I have met many retail store managers and owners who prize peace and harmony, among their employees, above all else. They simply cannot (or will not) handle employee conflicts and arguments. To a large degree, their hiring decisions are based on how well new employees will fit into the existing "team" rather than on how well they will perform with customers.

These managers have a tendency to consider "nice" as a desired, or even a required, quality for their new hires. Their floors are generally peaceful and quiet, but not necessarily very financially successful or productive.

The top managers tend to be on a different mission. Their working hours are spent focused on higher sales and profits, along with happier customers. They will inevitably select employment candidates with personality characteristics that support their mission.

Some personality traits are mutually exclusive. For example, you generally can't have a placid, quiet, timid individual who makes a great, friendly, out-going sales person.

Remember that the characteristics (R's & D's) you select for your <u>great</u> prospects should contribute to your mission (whatever you decide that mission will be).

Now, we have finished the preliminaries. It is time to put all of the secrets we have discussed to good use and find some great prospects.

Secret #16—Newspaper Want-Ads Are A Lousy Bet!

Want-ads in the local daily newspaper have been a mainstay of retail recruiting since people washed their clothes in the tub out back.

Sadly, the World has changed.

There are two problems with newspaper want-ads in the Twenty-first Century:

<u>Problem #1—What is Black & White and *Not* Read All Over?</u>

Statistics from the Audit Bureau of Circulations (whatever that is) indicate a steady decline in newspaper readership for at least the last decade. Average declines range from 3% to 5% per year. It isn't unusual for a large city newspaper to show a 10% to 15% drop in one year! In some cities, the <u>total</u> readership of a daily newspaper may be close to 10% of the population on a weekday.

When I speak with retail managers (which happens almost every day), it's not unusual to hear something like this:

Me: "Do you advertise in the paper when you need new associates?"

Manager: "Sure, if I can fit it into my budget. It's really expensive!"

Me: "Do you get any response from your ads?"

Manager: "Yeah! We get a huge response—lots of resumes and some drop-by's."

Me: "Are any of the applicants good?"

Manager: "Sometimes, but not usually."

Me: "Do you subscribe to the newspaper?

Manager: "Not at home. It comes to the store so we can see our sale ads."

This exchange leaves me with two questions:

> #1—If newspaper circulation is declining and "good" readership on a Sunday might be twenty-five percent of the total area population or less, what percentage of the total readership actually takes the time to read the "Employment" section? Do currently employed (happy or unhappy) workers take the time to read through the "want-ads" regularly?

> I have found no hard statistics to answer these questions. My personal guess is: a very small percentage of a newspaper's <u>total</u> (microscopically small) readership actually reads through the want-ads and the people reading the want-ads have a tendency to be the unemployed or the unhappy employees <u>only</u>.

#2—If the store manager doesn't take the newspaper at his/her home, why would he/she assume job prospects would take it?

Perhaps very few good applicants are coming from want-ads because few good applicants are actually reading the newspaper.

Once in a great while, I do hear about the complete opposite situation occurring.

From one small ad, the manager is flooded with applications.

Normally, this occurs in a town/city with extremely high unemployment and many of the applicants are looking for temporary jobs until the economy turns around or the local factory opens again.

In some ways, too many applications are worse than too few, especially if the majority of the applicants are unqualified, or uncommitted to a career in retailing. You have too many interviews and too few hires.

If this has happened to you, your job title suddenly changed from store manager to professional interviewer.

Problem #2—They All Look Alike!

I would like to make a prediction. Unlike the weatherman, who is making an educated guess, I <u>know</u> my forecast will be 100% correct, regardless the city in which you live.

This Sunday, the employment section in your local paper will be a blizzard of small, wordy ads desperately trying to stand out, but failing miserably. It will be a "black & whiteout" that can confound even the most determined job seeker.

Sure, you can try to "stand out" by spending thousands of dollars for a display ad, but you will still have "Problem #1" to solve and your incredibly expensive ad may still be overshadowed by other fancier, catchier ads.

If, on the other hand, you are blessed with a small/medium-sized city that sports few help-wanted pages every Sunday, you may be able to create good visibility, but can you be assured your best prospects are reading it?

The secret is that many top retail managers have given up on the newspaper want-ads totally. They use other techniques to locate great candidates. The techniques they choose allow their store to stand out from the crowd and screen out the less desirable prospects.

Secret #17—Successful Recruiting Messages Must Be:

If newspaper want-ads are no longer efficient recruiting tools (low visibility and high cost) what are the alternatives?

Good Question!!

We are about to discuss many options.

In order to gage the potential effectiveness of some new, unique prospecting techniques, we must first establish standards by which we will judge those systems.

In order to be considered "successful," a recruiting message must be:

Simple—uncomplicated

Visible to the "right" job prospects
(job prospects who have your Required and Desired Characteristics)

Unique from most other recruiting messages

Invisible to the wrong prospects (people who are not qualified by skills, character, habits, ability, appearance, etc.)

Cost effective—the results must justify the cost in time and money

Appealing and interesting

SECRET #18—CREATING "SUCCESSFUL" WANT-ADS!

Sorry to get you all excited. The truth is, "Successful" Daily Newspaper Help-Wanted Ad is an oxymoron (like "jumbo shrimp").

If you apply the standards above, you'll see that newspaper want-ads generally fail on at least five of the six standards.

In the Twenty-First Century, with few (very, very few) exceptions, newspaper want-ads are a waste of money, time and effort.

Does that sound harsh?

Just wait, it gets worse!

<u>If</u> you can do it, **<u>STOP</u>** using them, now, today!!

I know want-ads are part of the Status Quo! I know recruiting with want-ads is what we have always done! They are easy and quick (sometimes)!

I know that placing a want-ad makes you feel like you are doing something!

I know that placing a want-ad makes other people (bosses, supervisors, etc.) feel like you are doing something, too.

I also know they are expensive and they produce terrible results!

On top of that, the people who are reading the Employment Section of your newspaper are generally unemployed or unhappy with their current job. This translates into: "dissatisfied people."

Is that quality on your list of desired characteristics?

How about attracting stable, happy prospects that may not be "looking" at all? (We will talk more about this later.)

You will notice that I said, "<u>If</u> you can do it, **<u>STOP</u>** using them!!"

The operative word here is, "<u>If</u>." This is the real world!

In the real world, there are advertising contracts which must be honored or personal relationships (with local newspaper executives) which must be maintained.

In the real world, there are owners or corporate supervisors who think that the status quo must be maintained.

In the real world, sometimes, it just isn't possible to stop want-ads cold turkey.

If you are compelled (or think you are compelled) to continue want-ads in the local paper, here are some <u>secrets</u> that will minimize the total dollar outlays and maximize the potential impact of the ads:

Try to separate your ad from the blizzard. Go down to the newspaper and speak with a classified representative. Asking for help and ideas never hurts and it doesn't cost a thing, but <u>don't</u> fall for a sales pitch that raises the cost of your ad. Nothing you can do will make a huge difference.

—Unique appearance.

Ask what can be done in a want-ad at little or no additional cost. Ask about unique fonts (type style), unique type sizes (very small is best, very large will probably cost too much), special borders (look at the most common borders in last Sunday's paper and choose something different) or colors (not likely affordable, but you never know).

—Unique placement.

Ask how your ad can be placed at the beginning of a category (Retail, General, etc.) or at the top of the page. If it costs extra, skip it. Sometimes the ads are placed alphabetically by the first letter in the ad. If this is the case, you can modify your ad's verbiage to improve placement.

—Unique verbiage.

Try to say something different—something that attracts attention. Consider these examples:

"THANKS for a great year! Great people made the difference and we need a few more to fill out our team. If you want to join the top team in town, give us a call."

"How does your future look? If you are looking for an employer that shines brighter than all the rest, maybe we should talk!"

(or alphabetical to maximize placement at the beginning of the category)

"Aaaabsolutely incredible career growth opportunities! A five minute call can make a lifetime of difference!"

<u>Don't</u> use the "standard," "tried-and-true," "proven" language like, "immediate job opening," "inside sales," "now hiring," etc. It has been "proven" not to work.

<u>Don't</u> use blind ads! Most savvy job seekers will not respond to an ad that doesn't disclose a business name.

<u>Don't</u> ask for resumes. Ask applicants to come by in person. Many respondents for retail sales positions do not have resumes and cannot create one that looks decent.

<u>Don't</u> limit responses to a fax number and/or an e-mail address, unless familiarity with a fax machine or computer expertise is one of your D's. Many quality retail sales candidates do not have access to a fax or, believe it or not, a computer.

Secret #19—Use The Power Of Observation!!

Try this! It will save you time <u>and</u> money (which are, of course, the same)!!

Ask all job applicants to come into and <u>stay</u> at your store to fill out employment applications. If you don't use paper job applications (or virtual apps on a store computer), start NOW! Don't mail applications to prospects or allow them to be picked up and completed outside the store.

<u>All</u> job applications should be handed out by managers/owners, personally! Do not <u>ever</u> allow an application to be given out by a clerk, an office associate or a sales associate!!

If you cannot be in the store (day off or at lunch) no applications should be taken!

Here is the reason for this suggestion: THE POWER OF OBSERVATION!

If you, or another trusted management-type, give out the application, the applicant can be observed carefully.

<u>Does it matter</u> if the applicant—

- dresses like a slob, or a hooker, or a gangster?
- smells like a stockyard or an ashtray?
- doesn't smile?
- can't speak clearly?

- takes two hours to fill out a simple employment application?
- can't read or complete the job application without help?
- brings in a group of ten friends or, worse, ten children?
- is rude or inconsiderate?

Hmmm . . . Let me think.

If the applicants are losers, you don't have to waste your time interviewing them, regardless of the information on the application.

On the other hand, if they appear to be winners, you might take a minute to talk with them <u>before</u> they leave to put in an application at another store!

If you <u>do</u> decide to talk to a prospect, be friendly, SMILE, be positive and keep it short and to the point. If the prospect seems good or great, schedule a formal interview ASAP.

SECRET #20—THEY MAY BE BETTER THAN THE "DAILY NEWS!"

Almost every community has some specialty "newspapers." Many of them are available at no cost near supermarket/ drug store/restaurant entrances, or in boxes along city streets.

In general, specialty publications appeal to very limited and specific audiences: ethnic groups, senior citizens, antique buffs, theatre goers, young adults, gays and lesbians, political groups, suburbs, college/university students, military base residents, club members, etc.

The secret <u>advantages</u> of specialty periodicals (over the daily papers) as recruiting tools may be significant—

Lower cost—You may get more "bang-for-the-buck"; larger ads or more printings for the same or less expenditure.

Less competition—You may have fewer competitors for reader attention.

More "eyes"—Research indicates that, although fewer people are reading specialty publications, the people who <u>do</u> read them may read more of the total publication than readers of daily newspapers. In other words, specialty readers may be less likely to read just one section (sports, business, editorials, etc.) of the publication.

The <u>disadvantage</u> of specialty publications may be just as significant—

Guilt by association—Advertisement in specialty papers which espouse strong or controversial views may cause you and your store to be branded as sympathetic to those views. BE CAREFUL. Offending one group of customers in order to recruit from another group is NEVER worth it! Remain as neutral as possible, always.

Here are some secrets to success with specialty publications:

Select several possible publications in which to advertise. Pick up copies and READ them! Make sure they don't espouse extreme or heretical views that could damage your business' reputation.

Talk to the publishers to get information about circulation numbers and ad rates. Ask about demographics—who actually reads the paper and who the publisher wants to appeal to—target readership.

Ask yourself—Do the readers of this publication generally have qualities which appear on my list of D's. For example, if the readership of the publication is predominantly senior citizens and you are looking for young (18-25 year old) employees, it is definitely not the place to advertise.

Skip "Classified Ad" specialty publications. If the specialty newspaper is full of ads, why become just another ad? Remember, you are trying to make your message <u>unique</u>. You want to stand out from the crowd, not join it.

DO NOT sign any long-term advertising contracts! Insist on testing results before making <u>any</u> commitments!

Statistics are important!—KEEP THEM!

Circulation numbers from the publisher will undoubtedly be based on the number of papers published each day/week/bi-week, NOT on the number actually picked up and read. Take this information with a "grain of salt." When evaluating a publication consider looking at the distribution points (boxes) <u>just</u> <u>before</u> a new issue is distributed. Are the boxes empty or full? Empty boxes imply a strong readership, while full ones suggest few people pick the paper up and read it.

If you do decide to advertise in any specialty publication, keep careful track of two categories of results—total number of applications received as a result of the ad and the exact number of good or <u>great</u> applicants who apply (they have <u>many</u> of your D's). Hint, Hint, Hint: This is not a large numbers game! A few great, qualified applicants are better than a few dozen unqualified applicants.

We have already determined that daily newspaper want-ad's seldom work well! Stop using them if possible! Check out specialty publications. They may provide a viable and potentially effective alternative.

Secret #21—"Everyone" Doesn't Use Them!

Welcome to the Information Age.

Experts and techies (not necessarily the same) tell us, in a very loud and condescending way, that the World Wide Web (otherwise know as the Internet or just the Web) is "THE answer." They say, "In *the future*, <u>everyone</u> will search for a job using the Internet <u>only</u>."

I totally agree,

. . . but this is not *the future*! This is the present!

In the present, with a few exceptions, the internet is <u>not</u> the place to search for great new retail sales associates!

I wish that I could give you irrefutable statistics to prove this opinion, but I can't.

I can, however, tell you what some great store managers say—

— Locating a "good" job search web site is frustrating and confusing.
— There are dozens of mediocre or poor sites and many claims of great results.
— There appears to be little good information about which one's are best.
— Job posting fees can be high.

— Local job search sites (many sponsored by failing local newspapers) may lump your job posting into the middle of a blizzard of "work-at-home" offers making visibility limited.
— Actual results from retail sales associate postings have been <u>poor</u>, at best.

I can also tell you what some actual retail sales associates say

— They are unaware of or unfamiliar with internet job sites.
— Their Internet use, in many cases, has been limited to game, news and social sites. Many of them have told me that it never occurred to them to use the Internet to look for a job.
— Many do not have resumes and are intimidated by resume posting systems.

Okay, so when does the Internet work for retail job postings?

I honestly don't know.

I <u>do</u> know that many Internet job postings for professional positions (Engineers, IT Specialties, Medical Specialties, high ticket Sales) draw an avalanche of resumes.

Due to time demands, hiring authorities and HR people may only see a fraction of the resume responses before making a hiring decision. This makes Internet job searches less appealing to savvy candidates because their qualifications may never be seen by the people who matter.

At the moment, the Internet is, at best, a resume mill and, at worst, a black hole which can swallow your entire job search budget.

For now, the secret about Internet job sites is that it is best to skip them completely, unless you are willing to pay your new associates in the $100k range (if so, give me a call)!

Keep your eyes open, though. Maybe things will change in "the future."

Secret #22—TV And Radio Ratings Are Low!

Thus far, some secrets have been rather lengthy.

Good news! This is one won't take long.

The biggest challenge, in conducting a job search, is to get your message (the job opening) in front of as many <u>qualified</u> candidates as possible. At the same time, you have to avoid attracting poor candidates who will waste your time and theirs.

Top managers know that television and radio advertisements are too expensive and too random to be of real value in a retail sales associate search. This includes listings on a local television job program/channel (help-wanted ads scroll by occasionally). These television ads are often packaged with a newspaper want-ad and an internet job posting.

Effectively targeting your desired audience with this electronic media is more a matter of chance than of certainty. Regardless of what the TV/Radio salespeople may claim, they cannot guarantee that your job opening will reach the eyes and ears of your great candidates, EVER!

None of the store managers with whom I have worked have had any positive results from television, radio or packaged media job advertising packages.

No real secret—skip it. Spend your time and money in more productive ways!

Secret #23—It's A Sign That Nobody Wants To Work There!

"Help-Wanted/Now-Hiring" signs are often seen in retail store windows, on the sides of buildings, or free-standing in front of stores.

Like newspaper ads, they are part of the Status Quo.

Unlike newspaper ads, most of them are very cheap, and they <u>can</u> be quite effective—<u>if</u> they are noticed by the right people!

Here are some secrets and some "not-so-secrets" to creating effective "Help-Wanted and Now-Hiring" signs:

They have been used since the beginning of recorded history.

They are viewed as "low class" or trashy by many retailers.

They are simple, cheap, and passive recruiting tools.

They require little or no effort to create.

They are completely random search tools. While they may yield a small trickle of highly qualified candidates, they will often produce an ocean of poor prospects.

They provide undeniable proof that you (the store manager) are making an effort to find new people. (It gets the "boss" off your back and eases your conscience.)

Quick Reminder!!

Just so you don't forget.

Here are the standards by which "successful" recruiting techniques are measured:

APPEALING AND INTERESTING

SIMPLE

VISIBLE—to good prospects

UNIQUE

INVISIBLE—to bad prospects

COST EFFECTIVE—return on investment (ROI)

Before we apply the standards above to "Help Wanted/Now Hiring" signs, let's take a simple quiz.

Please fill in the blank:

"If _worst_ came to _worst_, and I _had_ to find a job, I _know_ I could _always_ find work at _____. They're _always_ looking for people!"

For most of us, the obvious answer is: convenience stores or fast food restaurants.

Question: How do you know that you could get a job at a convenience store or a fast food restaurant?

Answer: Because they <u>always</u> have "Help Wanted," "Now Hiring" or some other employment signage in their windows, on the side of their buildings or splashed across banners out on the street.

The signs are <u>permanent</u>. They have long since stopped attracting attention or presenting an effective message. No one really "sees" them anymore. They have simply become a part of the storefront.

Their actual message is:

"This is a bad place to work! We are always looking for people because no one stays with us very long!"

Now, to carry this idea a step further, go back to the test question and fill in the name of your store.

Guess what? If your store's "help wanted" signage is posted most of the time, it is just as effective and noticed as those at a local convenience store and fast food restaurant!!

I've got an idea! Let's avoid that dubious distinction!

Recruiting signs can work, <u>if</u> you follow the "Secret Rules."

Rules for <u>EFFECTIVE</u> Recruiting Signage—

Post signs TEMPORARILY and IRREGULARLY!! Put signs up for no more than one week at a time. After signs are removed, wait ten days before putting up a new one!

Use three different signs! Use one at a time. Use different colors and different words on each sign!

Place signs in different, <u>unique</u> locations—in window displays, beside registers, in merchandise displays, on delivery vehicles, on the roof, in restroom stalls, in dressing rooms, etc.

Keep the message SIMPLE! Don't try to put too much information on the sign. <u>Always</u> hint at scarcity—*"Only one opening!"* or *"Interviews this week only!"*

Say something unique! ***"This hasn't happened in a year!*** *We actually have an opening in sales! Apply now! It will be filled within two days!"*

The message of a help-wanted sign is more than the words on the sign. The secret to their success is to make them visible and to attract <u>positive</u> attention. Any other outcome will hurt your job search efforts.

Secret #24—Very Small, Unique Signs Can Work, Too!

Business cards are small signs which are used to promote a business or a professional. They have been used for a couple of centuries to provide information, including name, title and contact information. They are inexpensive, attract attention and easily fit in a pocket or a billfold (2" x 3 ½"). In spite of amazing advancements in technology, no better alternative has yet been devised.

Would it be possible to print a special message (other than name, address and phone number) on a standard-sized business card? Of course!

Consider this:

> **Thanks for smiling at me!**
>
> *Your attitude is a tremendous asset to your business!*
>
> *My business is looking for a person who smiles at customers. If you know someone who smiles like you <u>and</u> is looking for a great opportunity, I would love to talk to him/her.*
>
> *Have him/her call me—John Doe—(222) 444-5555*

Or this:

> *Every business in town is looking for excited, friendly, hardworking people!*

We already have some. But, we could use <u>one</u> more!

Know someone like this? Have them give me a call! They won't be disappointed!

John Doe—(222) 444-5555

There are <u>two</u> primary methods for distributing business card help-wanted "signs."

First is selective distribution. Although we will discuss this technique more fully in up-coming secrets, let it suffice to say that it involves handing the card directly to people who might know (or might be) actual job prospects.

The second method of distribution is broad and random. Business cards can be left on tables in waiting rooms, or handed to passing people on the street (or in the mall), or taped to gas pumps at the local gas station.

The first technique is highly effective and can yield great results. The card carries a personal message which means something to the individual receiving it. If the wording is done well, the card can give a strong compliment without looking like an attempt to steal another store's prize employee.

The second distribution method is potentially offensive and negative. Cards are given at random to individuals who may have little or no interest in the message, or they are left to trash up other peoples' property. If the cards are thrown down, your business may be blamed for the mess. If the cards are left out in the open, they may be trashed before a prospect actually looks at them.

A few years ago I went to a motivational sales seminar. A seasoned veteran of selling proudly explained his unique advertising system involving the random distribution of business cards. He would regularly attend minor league baseball games in his town. When his team hit a home run and everyone stood up to cheer, he would throw up a handful of his own business cards advertising him and his products. The cards would rain down like confetti in celebration of the dinger.

The sales pro thought this was the greatest idea in the world and it obviously got some customer attention for him. On the other hand, it trashed up the stadium more than normal, causing extra cleaning expenses. It also meant that people were walking over or sitting on his business' trash for the rest of the game (not a very positive image).

I would be the last person to stifle creativity. If you have an idea about randomly distributing a help-wanted message on business cards (or the flyers we will discuss later) and you think it will work, by all means try it. But remember, whenever you embark on a random recruiting technique it is <u>unlikely</u> to yield results which are significantly better than the newspaper, or a sign out in front of your store. Along with the prospects you want, you will also draw prospects who are hopelessly unqualified, but willing to waste more of your valuable time than they deserve.

Secret #25—Receipts Can Help!

Your customers can be excellent job prospects <u>and</u> prolific sources of candidate referrals.

One positive method of giving them the "now-hiring" message is to print it on your store's receipts or billing statements.

There are several options to consider.

Inexpensive—You might be able to personally enter a customized message into your register or printer which appears on every receipt.

Slightly more expensive and labor intensive—You can have a simple rubber stamp made. Every time a receipt or billing statement is generated the recruiting message can be stamped on the back (if the associate remembers to do it).

A little more expensive—You can buy specialized rolls of register paper or customized statements on which your recruiting message is imprinted.

Here are a few possible messages for receipts or statements:

> *We value people who are friendly, hardworking, and honest!*

> *We know you do too!*

We are looking for <u>one</u> of those people to join our sales team.

Please send us your friendly, hardworking, honest friends and family!

We would love to tell them about our opportunity.

Too long? How about this:

We need your help!

We need <u>one</u> friendly, hardworking, honest person to join our team.

Do you know of anyone who fits that profile? We would love to talk to them.

<u>Still</u> too long? Try this:

Thanks to you, business is good! We need one more person for our team.

Know someone who would be good? Call us.

Or, simply:

Time to grow! We need <u>one</u> person!
Know someone? Call us today.

How effective will these simple messages be? There is no good way to forecast. A simple, effective recruiting message printed on a customer's receipt or statement might be just enough to prompt the customer to remember a son or a daughter, a niece or a nephew, a friend or a friend's relative who is looking for a job.

What is the disadvantage of this technique?

It is random and potentially volatile.

Customer referrals can range from high quality to no quality at all. You are probably obligated to interview all referrals (regardless of qualifications) because they were referred by a customer. Also keep in mind that turn-downs must be handled carefully so that the referring customer is not offended that you wouldn't hire her son or daughter.

Secret #26—Wear Your Help-Wanted Sign!

T-shirts and ball caps have been popular for years. If they are imprinted with a clever or interesting message, they will be worn and <u>seen</u> by thousands of people.

No, I am not suggesting "help-wanted t-shirts!"

I am, however, bringing up the potential power of messages which are worn on clothing, like name tags and specialty buttons.

Our eyes are just naturally drawn to unique features of a person's wardrobe. Every time we see a name tag or a button our eyes move to read it.

This means that a recruiting message can easily be transmitted using employee name tags or specialty buttons.

As with all recruiting messages, it should be simple. It is even more important that badges and buttons transmit a message in the fewest possible words.

Here are a couple of examples:

Fun work can be rewarding!! Ask me how!

Work Here—Make Money

As with any other sign, the key to successful recruiting with name tags and buttons is to use them on an irregular basis. If your regular customers see them over and over they will stop noticing them.

Be prepared! The results of this technique will be random. Your effort could draw some great prospects, but it will also probably draw some terrible ones.

Secret #27—Productive Flyers, Not Another Oxy-Moron!

In our Specialty Business Cards discussion we talked about the disadvantages of randomly distributing <u>any</u> printed material (like business cards or flyers) to the public.

The trash generated could create a bad image of your business and the random nature of spreading flyers may not generate <u>any</u> of the desired results (good/great job prospects).

Then why do we need to discuss this matter further? I may have given you the idea that recruiting flyers are never of value and that isn't exactly accurate.

Here are three secrets to <u>productive</u>, <u>cost-effective</u> flyers:

First—If you are looking for a new employee who lives close to your store, or if you are trying to recruit students from a particular school, you may want to consider flyers. In a relatively small area (a subdivision, an apartment building or a school), flyers announcing a job opening can be cost effective and attention-grabbing.

Second—Attractive, colorful flyers may attract the attention of job seekers if they are posted on bulletin boards that job seekers are looking at: high schools, college dorms, college "job boards," church or grocery store bulletin boards, etc. For years, flyers with telephone number tear-offs at the bottom have sold everything from houses to harp lessons. Why not job openings?

Third—Flyers may also be used as inserts in specialty newspapers. Sometimes it is cheaper (and significantly more effective) to place an insert in a small specialty newspaper than it is to place a display advertisement, especially if you do the printing and all they have to do is insert the flyer. Shop around. Be innovative.

In order to improve the success of any flyer, be sure that it is printed on <u>white</u> paper, NOT colored paper. Colored ink is okay, but the cost will probably be prohibitive. Keep the message simple and direct.

Why white paper? Over the years, the public has overused and misused colored paper. Official notices and important letters are always written on white paper. If your flyer is placed in door handles or in mail boxes, colored flyers are dispatched quickly as junk mail. White flyers have a better chance of being examined before they are trashed.

Oh, I almost forgot. We also need to discuss mail-outs.

SECRET #28—TWO EXCEPTIONS TO THE "NO MAIL RULE!"

Good news, this will be short and sweet! Mail-outs cost too much (even pre-sort) and are too random to be of any value. As a general rule, you shouldn't waste your money mailing out job opening announcements to the public.

There are, however, two secret exceptions to the rule!

#1—If you have a <u>solid</u> mailing list—like a list of employees being laid off at a bankrupt business or a list of all high school seniors in your area—a mail-out <u>might</u> work.

#2—If you can add a flyer or a specialty business card to a mailing that is going out anyway—monthly statements or product brochures—you can piggy-back off of a previously budgeted mailing expense. Be careful, though, you don't want your postage costs per piece to increase because the flyer has been added.

Secret #29—Finally, Something That Works!

Thus far, we have talked about recruiting techniques which provide varying levels of success—from expensive, ineffective newspaper want ads to inexpensive, occasionally effective signs and flyers.

Now it's time to talk about a technique that actually works well <u>all</u> of the time (<u>if</u> it is used consistently).

Its cost is generally negligible and it requires little or no major time investment.

If done correctly, it is truly magic.

Okay, so why would anyone refer to networking as "magic," you ask?

The process of networking can produce qualified, interested, excited candidates who <u>want</u> to work for your business. But that's not all!

It can also enhance your store's reputation in the community and bring in new customers (who have never visited your store before).

All of this can be done for a total dollar investment of $0.00!!

Does it all sound too good to be true?

Well, I have good news for you. It is very, very real!

Here are some of the secrets about help-wanted networking:

— It works best with a simple message, nothing fancy. Amazing results occur when it is done casually.

— Get started by speaking <u>directly</u> to the people who have the "desired" qualities you are looking for, or people might know great prospects.

— Consistent networking, done honestly and with tact, produces consistent results.
   Occasional networking may not produce any results at all. In a way, it's like priming a hand pump. Once the water starts to flow, you must keep pumping steadily. If you stop, the flow stops and you have to prime the pump again!

— Networking not only gets your help-wanted message out into the community, it also causes your business' name to be mentioned repeatedly to prospective customers.

— The most successful networkers are quick to say "thanks" to their referral sources.

This is done with good communications and bonuses like a store discount, a monetary reward or just a simple note/e-mail. You get to decide what works best for you.

SECRET #30—VERTICAL NETWORKING IS BEST!

There are three basic forms of networking.

First is <u>random</u>. This type of networking occurs when you mention your job openings to just about everyone—your doctor, your minister, your friends, people you meet, people who serve you in stores and restaurants. This exercise works sometimes, but it is hit-or-miss, at best. Generally, as with all other random methods of recruiting, it is a WASTE OF TIME and energy. It often annoys people and turns them off. Skip it!

Second is <u>horizontal</u>. This occurs when contacts are developed within one particular industry or organization. For example, if you regularly talk with other store managers or owners about business matters, you are networking horizontally.

Third is <u>vertical</u>. When you develop several contacts in other non-competitive businesses or organizations who share information and insights with you, you are networking vertically.

Although horizontal networking can be very effective, the secret is that vertical networking consistently yields the best recruiting results.

The objective of a recruiting network is to build a group of business professionals or centers-of-influence who refer good/great job candidates to you, when you need them.

In order for this arrangement to be successful your network members need to like you, trust you and believe in your project (locating job prospects). As I mentioned earlier, they need to be rewarded with good communication (follow-up), honesty, reliability, proper treatment of their referrals and heaps of honest appreciation. They need to <u>know</u> that referring their friends and contacts to you is the <u>right</u> thing to do!!

Building a good recruiting network may require some time. Be patient. Be diligent. Don't get anxious or pushy! Allow members to officially join your network of contacts when <u>they</u> feel comfortable.

Keep in mind that an effective recruiting network is <u>on-going</u>. It isn't created from scratch each time your store has an opening. A network should be developed and maintained for immediate availability whenever a job opening occurs.

The size of your network can vary, but, most of time, a maximum of five or six members yields the best results. The choice is, of course, yours, but with the managers and recruiters with whom I have worked, the more members in the network, the more likely that someone will be forgotten or offended by poor follow-up. Remember, screw-ups (even accidental screw-ups) are costly in networking.

Secret #31 — Pre-Qualify The Members Of Your Network!

In order for a professional or a center-of-influence to be considered a good prospective member of your network, he/she should have three qualities.

First, (oh, duh) the person must consistently talk to, run into, meet or otherwise work with people who might meet your qualifications for "good" or "great." It also doesn't hurt if they know people who are looking for a new job opportunity. Not just any job, but a job like those available in your store!

Second, the person must CARE! They _must_ be truly interested in helping the job prospects they run into. I know this seems obvious, but it is worth considering. A person can be a center-of-influence by job title, but they may not be willing to go out of their way to actually help _anyone_. For example, there may be a high school or college counselor who talks to students who need jobs all the time, but if they won't take the time to refer them to you, the counselor is of no value and should be avoided.

Third, the person must take an interest in you and your business. This one is a little more complex than the previous two. You want the members of your network to send you prospects who meet _your_ basic hiring criteria. If your network member is interested in you and your business, they respect you and they will send prospects who are well suited to your business and the opening which you have described to them. If they are not interested, they will send every warm body that fogs a mirror. Wading through a seemingly endless line of poor prospects is time consuming and, therefore, a waste of money. You can't afford it!

The secret here is—Get to know the members of your referral network and let them get to know you. Instead of just asking them for referrals, let them know who you are looking for and why. Tell them about your goals and give them information about your business. Remember, you are actually creating a referral "team."

Who do you want on your team? Select carefully!

Secret #32—Friends? Current Employees? Be Careful!

<u>Friends</u>

Have you ever had a friend who "knows everyone," a social gadfly who loves meeting, talking to and knowing as many people as possible? This type of person might be a great choice for network member. They like people. They like helping people. They like you.

Be careful, though. Friendships can be delicate. You don't want to offend an overly sensitive friend because you didn't hire their referral.

Friends (and other recruiting network members) should be warned up front that you will make hiring decisions based on the best interest of your store and information used in your hiring decision cannot always be disclosed to them due to privacy laws.

<u>Current Employees</u>

Here is a classic "double-edged sword."

Employees can be good, <u>occasional</u> sources of job prospects, BUT always remember the "birds-of-a-feather" quote.

Here is a secret we generally ignore "Birds-of-a-feather flock together."

It means, of course, that people tend to hang around (socialize) with those who share common views, beliefs and habits. We are all more comfortable when we are around people who are like us.

Top employees, who are timely, hardworking, honest and friendly, tend to hang around people who are similar to themselves. Poor employees, who have poor habits, or major character flaws, (drinkers or stoners, for example) tend socialize with people who make them feel comfortable—people with similar habits or character flaws.

Here is that double-edged sword. If we can assume that good employees will refer good job prospects to the store and bad employees will refer bad job prospects to the store, then it doesn't make any sense to ask all of your employees for referrals, unless all of your employees are good/great. Sorry, I'm not buying that.

Remember, bad job referrals (defined as, those who do not meet your criteria for a good/great prospect) are a WASTE of your time and your money. Interviewing them does not lead to a positive outcome!

In order to maximize the potential of employee referrals, talk to good employees privately. Compliment them and reassure them that they are a valuable member of your employee team. Explain who you are looking for and why ("why" is very important). Then ask for their help in the form of referrals. Ask them not to discuss your conversation with other employees on the floor.

Employee referrals carry an inherent risk. It is always possible that a good employee could refer a buddy or a "significant other," to you. If you hired them, they could become a major distraction to the original good employee. Close friendships on the sales floor can also aggravate other employees and lower morale. In situations like this, one job opening might turn into two or more in short order.

Current employees probably won't be the most productive members of your referral network. They may know a few people who are looking for job, but probably not many. It is probably best to use good/great employee referrals occasionally, but not for every opening.

Secret #33—Customers—Handle With Care!

On the surface, good customers seem like naturals in your referral network.

This is a tough call, but the secret is it's probably not a good idea. It may turn out to be more trouble than it's worth.

Of course, you would be hard-pressed to find better cheerleaders for your business. Good customers like your products, like your employees and like your way of doing business. They probably wouldn't intentionally send you any referrals who might hurt your business.

On the other hand, customers are like friends. They might become offended because you <u>didn't</u> hire their referral and you might not be able to tell them why.

They also might become offended because you <u>did</u> hire their candidate and the new employee became disillusioned for one reason or another. An experience like this could turn a good customer into a former customer.

Thanks, but no thanks.

It is also difficult to tell which customers might know people who are looking for a job. This leads to the old problem of random requests for referrals and the inevitable poor results such a request generates.

Unless you know a customer who constantly comes into contact with good prospects (teacher, counselor, etc.), it probably doesn't make much sense to use them in your recruiting network. Let the interested customers make referrals based on their notice of the "help wanted" signs which occasionally (very occasionally) show up in your store.

Secret #34—Schools Are A Big Hit!!

Schools can be an <u>excellent</u> source (maybe the BEST source) of referrals and referral network members. Depending on your skills in selecting referral network members, they could also be a very bad source.

When evaluating the potential for schools in your area, here are some things to keep in mind:

Before approaching <u>anyone</u> in a school, take a minute to review your list of desired characteristics for a great employee.

Which students are the best prospects for your business?

Does your vision of a great employee include a perfect age range? Are you looking for young (high school age), slightly more mature (college age), or significantly more mature (adult continuing education <u>or</u> school teachers themselves). Does age matter at all?

Are you looking for individuals with special skills (business schools)?

Are part time candidates of interest or do you need full time only?

Your best potential referral sources see many students who need jobs. These educators want to help their students and can learn to like your business, if you give them a chance.

In return for their generosity, you must treat their students fairly, keep them informed and show your appreciation for their help. That is, if you want the referrals to continue.

Here is an important secret about educators. Principals, teachers, and other instructors, in <u>larger</u> schools, may not always be your best networking contacts. Remember, you want to build relationships with the professionals who work closely with your top prospects and are aware of your prospects' need for work.

In very large schools, the principals may see only the worst students (behavioral problems, truants, etc.). The teachers in these schools see large groups of students, but they may not have the time to discuss extracurricular activities (jobs after school) with most of them.

High school guidance counselors may be good possibilities. Similarly, placement advisors or course advisors in colleges/business schools may be productive referral sources. Some of them even get actively involved in helping students locate summer and after school employment.

Some high schools have coordinators who help students go to school part time and work full/part time. Sometimes these work/school relationships will earn special course credits for the students.

In very <u>small</u> schools (private or public) administrators may turn out to be your best source of help. In some of these institutions, the principals do everything—discipline, instruction and counseling.

Don't forget the clerical and support staff! In many schools, the secretaries and administrative assistants can be an excellent source of information about job candidates. They may have daily conversations with students on a more casual basis than other school employees.

Another potentially productive source of referrals might be a teacher/advisor for specific after-school clubs and organizations (business clubs, etc.).

Even if you can't find a good network source within a local school, you might be allowed to post a recruiting flyer in the teachers' lounge or on a student activity bulletin board. You might also be allowed to distribute flyers in teacher mail boxes.

Here are some secrets to help you establish a school-based relationship.

Always call before you go by a school. Ask to speak with a particular individual, like a guidance counselor or a placement adviser. Be patient; be honest; be open about your objectives. I have found that most school administrative and clerical employees are easy enough to work with if you ask for their help and don't try to be too pushy. They will start out suspicious, but as time goes by and you prove yourself, their insights and assistance will flow.

To build confidence in your business, you can always invite your potential network sources to come by your store. You can let them talk directly with your good/great associates about the store culture and working conditions.

No secret—don't ever let your visitors talk to the bad or the unhappy employees who might say negative things!

Secret #35—These Resources Could Be A Blessing!

There are literally thousands of different religious groups and organizations. For the purpose of our discussions, I am going to refer to them all as "churches." Please do not take this reference in offense. You can read it as mosque, synagogue, temple, tabernacle or any other appropriate terminology.

Churches can be an excellent place to develop new members of your vertical recruiting network and locate job prospects. Interested church members and professionals can help you find young prospects, old prospects and everyone in between.

In the network recruiting process, churches are similar to schools. Depending on the size of the congregation, the worship leader may not be your most productive contact.

A church secretary or staff member will generally be a good source of information. He/she will be able to give you ideas about teachers/lay leaders/counselors who might know church members who would appreciate a new job opportunity.

The secret to recruiting through religious institutions is to recognize that you don't have to be of a specific faith to build a prospect referral relationship in a church. Think outside of your own comfort zone. For this project, consider putting your personal views and beliefs aside. You are looking for

<u>great</u> new job candidates, not necessarily people of a specific faith or denomination (unless a particular religion is one of your desired qualities). You have something of real value to offer the members of the church—a job!

Although there are extraordinary benefits from recruiting within a religious organization there can also be hazards. If your store sells shoes or clothing, there may be no conflict. On the other hand, it goes without saying, if your store sells cigarettes, liquor or adult entertainment items, churches may not be the best source for new sales associates.

Secret #36—Smaller Service and Civic Clubs Are Generally Forgotten!

If you have been thinking ahead about building a vertical recruiting network, it has probably already occurred to you to consider working with members of some large civic and service organizations, like the Optimist Club, the Rotary Club, the Kiwanis Club, etc.

Frankly, contacts within many of the largest service groups will probably yield few good prospects, unless you are interested in the sons and daughters of the members. Most of the members of these clubs are established business professionals within your community who may not be interested in sending you job prospects.

This is not, however, the case with all service organizations or clubs.

Consider these "secret" organizations:

Veterans Organizations (DAV, VFW, etc.)—a good source of seasoned citizens

Senior Citizens Groups—goes without saying

Hobby and Sport Groups—a possible source of youths or seasoned citizens

Fraternal Organizations—another source of seasoned citizens

Why are these groups "secret?" No one ever thinks to contact them. Remember that even if you aren't looking for the older crowd, they may have children and grandchildren who would benefit from a job in your store.

There are literally hundreds of groups that could be a regular source of job prospects.

Secret—Consider working with organizations that might use your store's products—a dog breeders association for a pet products store or a quilting club for a fabric store.

Remember, you are looking for people who know and talk to lots of other people. If you can't find a good potential member for your network, you can always ask to post your openings on the organization's bulletin board (for free) or advertise it (for a nominal fee) in the group's monthly newsletter.

Secret #37—Spouses Are Prospects!

This source of members for your recruiting network (and job seekers) is near and dear to my heart. The brave men and women of our armed forces are held in high esteem for the work that they do.

The secret is that their spouses are often ignored. Some of them could be <u>great</u> employees in your store!

If there is a military installation in your area, there may be a surprisingly large, untapped reservoir of talent which is waiting for you to express an interest.

As with "churches," I will warn you at the beginning of our discussion, I am going to refer to all military installations as "bases." I understand that there are also posts, camps, forts, yards and other terms. For brevity, one name will refer to all places military.

Depending on the number of military personnel stationed on the base(s) near you, there may be an office to help military spouses find work. Generally, the services provided by these offices are free to employers and job seekers.

It makes sense to develop contacts in these spousal placement offices and to make them part of your network.

There are two ways of handling relationships with placement services (whether military or private).

The first is passive. You can give the people in the placement office your name and information and then sit around and wait for a call.

On the other hand, it is a well-kept secret that you can take a more pro-active, assertive role. You can visit the placement office and get to know the people who are working there. You can also invite them to visit your store (Oops, new customers!) and let them meet your employees.

The active role may not produce significantly better results than the passive role, but there is a chance that your interest and support for the base services will be rewarded in other ways (like new customers).

On smaller bases, there is probably won't be any placement office for spouses, but there probably will be spousal support groups that meet regularly to help the spouses of deployed personnel. Relationships with these organizations might lead to some excellent candidate referrals.

Here is a secret that most recruiters never consider. Every military facility has some type of relocation/housing office that assists military families in the process of moving from or to a new base. If you can meet and talk to the housing personnel, you might find that they too will be glad to help you attract spouses who are interested in working in retail.

If you are unfamiliar with the military, it may seem like a daunting task to get started on this type of networking.

Don't be intimidated. On military bases, many of the people with whom you speak meet the criteria for being included in your vertical recruiting network. They are normal people who are doing important work and genuinely appreciate your interest.

My advice is to pick up the phone and call anyone and everyone who might work with you. Be humble, tell them that you know little, or nothing, and ask for their help.

If you decide to go out to the local military facility, be prepared to show proof of insurance and a picture id at the gate. Tell the guard exactly where you would like to go (housing office, placement office, etc.) and why.

You will be surprised at the results your simple actions can generate—QUICKLY.

Secret #38—Don't Write Off The Competitors—Yet!

Although it's always easier to network within vertical groups which have non-competitive interests (schools, churches, clubs, military), it may also be possible to develop productive networking within horizontal groups of competing businesses.

In general, horizontal relationships require more time and patience to build than other arrangements. Trust is the main issue.

I know! I know! You are thinking, *"You've got to be kidding! My competitors would never give my store a halfway decent prospective employee!!"*

Maybe.

Maybe not.

You never know until you ask.

Here is the secret truth:

You probably have some type of limited contact with your competitors already. Most store managers/owners do. Maybe it's a phone conversation every once in a while to scrounge for information and to chit-chat. Maybe it is an occasional stop-by to check out the other store's traffic and merchandise displays and to chit-chat.

If your relationship with a competitive store is rocky or contentious, or if you don't talk to them at all, forget this idea altogether.

Here is the horizontal networking secret—If communication with a competing store is friendly, ask the manager if they are looking for new associates. If they are, forget it, they would only send you their rejects anyway. But, if they <u>aren't</u> looking for new people, they might send walk-ins over to your store, instead of sending them on their way. This is particularly effective if the competing store is on the other side of your town (some distance away).

In order to make this simple idea work, you must stay on good terms with your competitors and you must offer to reciprocate (return the favor) when you have filled your store with great employees.

Admittedly, this is a <u>weak</u> source of job prospects, at best, but it is a source none-the-less. A competitor would never be in your vertical network, but developing a good relationship with him/her might pay surprising dividends.

Secret #39—Don't Write Off The Non-Competitors—Yet, Either!

Let me ask you, do you shop or use services?

Do you shop for groceries, buy gasoline, shop for clothes, have your clothes cleaned or get your teeth drilled (hopefully not often)?

The answer is, "Of course!" And everyone you buy products or services from is a "retailer."

I know this seems painfully obvious, but some of us forget.

The idea of horizontal networking with non-competitors is very similar to working with competitors and it isn't totally random.

Take just a moment to network as you shop. Get to know the manager(s) and tell them the name of your store. Invite them to come by.

As your relationship builds, ask the non-competitor/manager to refer job prospects to your store if his store is not currently hiring. He/she may also be willing to refer prospects who do not meet his/her qualifications for a good/great prospect, but do meet yours (older, younger, different physical capabilities, etc.).

This may seem like a silly idea, but you might be surprised at the outcome. Even if you don't see any referred job prospects, you might get a new customer.

That pretty much takes care of networking. It's time to consider recruiting opportunities created by tragedies.

Secret #40—A Wreck Can Be Good For Your Store!

Keep your eyes open. Watch for "Going Out of Business," "Liquidation Sale," "Store Closing" or "Bankruptcy Sale" signs. If you actually read the newspaper, or listen to the local news on TV or radio, pay attention to stories about businesses (all types of businesses) closing their doors.

This is obviously not good news (unless it is one of your direct competitors)! Your city or community is about to lose an employer.

On the other hand, if you are looking for good prospects you might be in luck.

Here's the secret (and it's a <u>great</u> secret!). As soon as you see one of the indicators of a business wreck, DON'T WAIT. Go to the business and ask to speak to the store/general manager, business manager or human resources manager.

You will probably find him/her <u>very</u> interested in talking to you. He/she probably wants the displaced employees to find new jobs as soon as possible.

Explain that you have an opening and you would like to interview any interested employees, if possible, <u>at the failing store or business, before or after normal business hours</u>. If you want to impress the manager of the business, explain that you are not thinking of taking any employee away until after the bankruptcy sale or business closing is completed.

Businesses which have run aground due to poor financial management or have crashed on the rocks of a bad economy offer a tremendous opportunity to find quality associates.

Remember to act fast!

Even before the word gets out that their business is going under, employees may have started looking for new employment. If you don't get there soon enough, everyone will be gone.

Secret #41—Maintain Your Standards!!

The list of required and desired characteristics (R's & D's) that you made earlier is more than just a list. It is a clear statement of your personal hiring standards. It is a direct reflection of the qualities that you value in yourself and in your employees! It shouldn't be taken lightly! And it should be used every time you begin a recruiting project or interview a prospect.

When you are recruiting or interviewing employees who have just seen their company go under, you will be talking to sad, confused, lost and even angry people. Don't let your personal sympathy for their plight affect your judgment.

MAINTAIN YOUR STANDARDS!

You don't represent a charitable organization. You will not help your store by hiring a failed business' weak employees.

To facilitate your efforts, and avoid major mistakes, you can review your list with the manager of the closing business and ask his/her advice about employees who might meet your criteria.

The important thing is to stay on course. You have something of value to offer. Don't give it away to someone because you feel sorry for them.

Secret #42—Co-Op's Can Yield Dividends!

I bet you thought that my suggestion about talking to competitors was about as weird as I could get! Think again!

As the name implies, a hiring co-op is a group of employers who have bound together to find good job prospects.

This idea is most commonly seen when two or more stores within the same franchise organization or company work together to share advertising/recruiting costs. Believe it or not, it can also work with unrelated competitive and non-competitive retailers in the same market.

Here's the idea:

You form a group of retailers (two or more).

The participants agree on a recruiting technique that would otherwise be prohibitively expensive for one retailer acting alone (a full page ad in specialty newspaper, an ad in a professional sports program, an electronic billboard, a television ad during the Super Bowl, etc.).

The participants create and agree on a snappy recruiting message and split the cost of the advertisement.

Here is the catch. All participants must be honest and they <u>must</u> trust each other.

The advantage of the technique is obvious. It puts your business' name in places it might not otherwise appear.

The disadvantage is also obvious. It deludes your recruiting message by lumping it in with several others.

There are a couple of common techniques for handling job seekers who respond to your co-op recruiting effort.

> Each retailer can be listed separately in the recruiting message giving every member of the co-op an equal chance to receive responses.

> Respondents can be directed through a central "clearinghouse" that gives the job seekers resumes/applications to <u>all</u> stores, or one store at a time, in order.

Although I am not a strong proponent of the hiring or recruiting co-op idea, I can see its advantages in creating visibility that would otherwise not be available. As long as the participants can make decisions without bickering and in-fighting, the potential results might make the effort worth the trouble.

SECRET #43—EMPLOYMENT AGENCIES DON'T ALWAYS MAKE RECRUITING EASIER!

Employment agencies come in two basic varieties, government-funded and private.

Government Employment Agencies

Government employment agencies are generally funded by a state or municipal government and paid for with tax dollars.

This is good news and bad news!

The good news is that the services of government-funded employment agencies are free from direct dollar costs, most of the time. If there are costs to employers, they are probably very low.

The bad news is that many government employment agencies are riddled with bureaucracy and can be ponderous to work with. Services may be incredibly slow and paperwork might be overwhelming!

And worst of all, a government employment agency may be totally incapable of screening the good candidates from those who are hopelessly unqualified. Interviewing dozens of worthless or disinterested candidates can make finding one good candidate just too costly.

Is it possible (and beneficial) to build a networking relationship with a worker at your state employment service? You are going to have to make that judgment call for yourself.

During my career (twenty plus years of recruiting), I have had very little luck in building good working relationships with job placement bureaucrats. In my experience, they are generally more interested in sending out ex-convicts and ex-addicts (not on my list of preferred characteristics) for interviews than sending me the perfect job candidate.

Does that sound cynical? Excellent!! That is exactly what I intended.

There are undoubtedly some dedicated, caring, hardworking bureaucrats who can help you find the right associate for your store. I just never found any!

Private Employment Agencies

In my experience, there are three primary types of private employment agencies. These are my classifications, not theirs.

#1—Temporary/Temp-to-Hire

Temporary employment agencies tend to specialize in three primary job classifications—clerical, manual labor and health care.

The concept here is simple. You need someone today and we will rush someone over ASAP. The original concept was to provide help for a limited period of time—a few hours to a few weeks.

In most cases, these agencies work with prospects who fulfill basic job skill requirements. The employer might be looking for individuals who can type or use a "10-key." The employer might need someone who has experience as a care-giver in a long-term care environment. The employer might need a breathing human being who can lift 50 pounds.

In most cases, temporary agencies do not seem to draw prospective placements (job applicants) who are looking for retail sales positions. If I find an agency that claims to provide my type of candidate, most of the time, I wind up with an endless parade sales prospects with none of my most desired characteristics (smokers; full body tattoos; multiple, visible piercings; unprofessional or poorly maintained hair, etc.).

Obviously there are exceptions. Some of the retail managers with whom I have worked enjoy judging a daily "beauty contest." Any time they have an opening, they call the temp agency and have a candidate, or four, sent over. If the prospect(s) does beautifully, he/she wins a full time job. The managers pay the agency's fee and make the temp an employee of their store. If the temp does poorly, he/she is not invited back for another day at the store.

Does this tactic work? Seldom. Even if your business can assimilate the cost, there is the issue of time. Sometimes it takes six or more temps who don't make it in order to find one that does. Training new people to be "functional" on your floor (notice I didn't say "beneficial") takes time.

Monitoring them and assessing their value as an employee takes more time. Lots more time!

Of course you do save time by avoiding the interview process, but what happens when you find a good temp who has a surprise in their background (a minor shoplifting conviction in the past)? You may not find it out until you are ready to hire. You have wasted a lot of time if the surprise is a deal-breaker.

This brings up the biggest disadvantage of the temp-to-hire process—COST. Most temp agencies charge an hourly fee for the temp, plus a placement fee if you decide to hire them. If you go through four or five temps before you find a "good" hire you might be looking at a large bill. The hourly rate for temps is generally more than you pay your employees. Remember that the temp fee includes the person's hourly pay, taxes, benefits and the hourly fee for the agency. It can be substantial.

It is difficult to get temp agencies to do any serious screening. Many of them are built to provide acceptable (not good, not great) temporary employees fast. Even when quick isn't so important, the temps seldom rise above the "acceptable" level.

It may appear that I am underwhelmed by temp agencies. I am. For retail sales hiring, I don't think they are worth the time or the money.

#2—Fee-for-Service

The employment agencies that I call "fee-for-service" are occasionally operated in coordination with a temp agency. Applicants may be charged a fee to be registered at the agency or they will be charged when they accept a job from a client employer. To attract better prospects the employer may agree to pay the employment agency fee.

Although my contact with these agencies has been limited, I have known many business people who attempted to use their services.

Fees can be substantial. This may become a challenge in several ways.

You, as the employer, may be required to deduct a portion of the new employee's pay to remit to the employment agency. This adds cost and record keeping challenges to the already expensive process of payroll.

It may make it hard to terminate an employee who doesn't "work out" and hasn't finished paying his/her placement fees. There may be penalties or nonrefundable portions of the placement fee.

The real challenge with fee-for-service employment agencies is their limited pool of candidates. From what I can tell, these agencies throw open their doors and wait on candidates to just come wandering in. There is some minor effort to attract good candidates with newspaper ads, but we all know how that works out. Most of the time, little or no effort is made to go out and find quality prospects.

What this means to you as an employer is simple. If you decide to risk the time and money involved in a fee-for-service recruiting adventure, you would be better served working with an experienced agency that has been in business in your town for a while. What's a "while?" Good question! I would say three to five years minimum.

Before you use any temp service or fee-for-service employment agency, you should ask around. Ask your business friends and competitors. Ask the agency for references. If they are any good, they should be able to get you the information quickly and easily.

#3—"Headhunters"/Professional Recruiters

Search firms, or "headhunters" are serious recruiting organizations. A business gives the firm a "job order" which includes detailed explanations of job duties, descriptions of great prospects and salary ranges.

Once the headhunter has enough information, he/she literally begins calling around to locate individuals who meet the specifications. The prospects are interviewed by the headhunter first, to screen for general suitability. Then the hiring company conducts interviews.

Once a person is hired, a fee is charged to the hiring company. It is normally based on a percentage of the new hire's first year income.

Search firms warrant little of our time. The firms are efficient and very professional. They are also <u>very</u> expensive.

If you are looking for high-end sales associates who will make high incomes ($100k+), a search firm makes a world of sense. The people you are looking for do not read the want-ads and are generally working happily for a competitor. In most cases, the only way to locate them is by professional recruiting efforts.

If, on the other hand, you are looking for someone who is a little lower on the food chain, skip the executive search firms.

It is important to note though that the headhunters have some useful and very effective recruiting techniques that they can teach us. We will discuss one of their methods later.

Secret #44—Go For More Party And Less "Beauty Contest!"

For years, companies have thrown caution to the wind and opened their doors wide so that prospective employees could walk in and examine their business, no holds barred.

Of course, in retail, the doors are already open wide, most of the time. It may make the concept of an "open house" seem a little redundant.

There are two sides of concept to consider (Boy, is that surprising!):

On the positive side, the concept of an employment open house in retail may be unique and totally unexpected in your area. To some, it may seem less threatening than walking in cold to answer an ad (although that seems a little timid). Because of the unique nature of the event it could draw more attention than some of your normal recruiting efforts.

On the not-so-positive side, here are the challenges I have observed:

First is publicity. How do you get the word out about your open house? It is pretty much the same problem you face with recruiting in general. The newspaper doesn't work. TV and radio are too costly for the people you reach. You can always put up signs on your building or on the street, but will anyone notice?

Can it actually be done? Sure, but it will take a special effort to get the word out and be sure to loosen the strings on your pocketbook. My advice would be to use signs <u>and</u> invitations mailed or delivered to schools and/or organizations (including churches). Your network of contacts could also help to make your event a success.

<u>Second</u> is the empty room. Most open houses start out like your holiday parties. No one wants to be first to arrive. When people come by, will they look in and see lots and lots of MT? If you have a rush from the beginning, the world is good. But it may be a real challenge to get things going, before people start walking off rather than walking in.

How do we get past the "empty room?" Simple, fill it up. Put as many people as possible in the room, milling around. Don't have people sitting behind tables. Get your current employees to attend and stand around and talk. The bigger the crowd the better chance you have to build a crowd!

To increase attendance numbers further, you can also invite the members of your vertical recruiting network to the open house. It is a great opportunity to give them tours of your store and introductions to members of your associate team.

Be sure someone is prepared to greet job prospects as soon as they walk in the door. They need to be noticed, welcomed and directed into the event ASAP after they walk in the door. This will avoid that "lost" feeling that turns everyone off.

To help draw people, you should always serve food. This can be a great incentive if it is used right. There is nothing wrong with offering a light dinner (burgers, tacos, etc.) for applicants who are getting off work.

It may make more sense to have the open house in the morning, <u>before</u> most retailers open. You can provide coffee, orange juice and small breakfast sandwiches/tacos and applicants can stop by on their way to their current job. Tip: Start at 7:00 am (For those people who have 8:00 to 5:00 jobs!) and finish about 10:00 am.

Don't worry about providing a lot of food variety! You can't please everyone.

Here are some great tips to insure a successful "Open House:"

— Don't serve any alcoholic beverages of any kind!!! It doesn't matter if it is "just" beer or wine or whatever! Don't do it! The liability is too great. It may draw a crowd, but for all of the wrong reasons.

— Offer food and drink <u>first</u>! Then talk employment. When people feel good and relaxed, conversations about jobs come more naturally. Don't make people feel like they have to fill out an application to qualify for the food you are providing.

— Hold your "open house" at someone else's "house." Another location might make your event look more "party" and less recruiting "beauty contest."

You could have it at a restaurant, at a community meeting room or even at someone's home (Make sure it is nice, clean and signs are clearly posted. By the way, is it handicap accessible?). You could even have a cookout at a local park (serving hotdogs, potato chips and sodas)! It should be easy to get to and as non-intimidating as possible.

— In most cases, hotels and professional meeting rooms are impersonal, expensive and may drive prospects away. Skip them!!

— Keep conversations with prospects friendly, light and fluffy. Don't get bogged down in full-blown interviews. Gather information (applications and resumes); ask a few important questions and schedule interviews with prospects who appear to meet your R's and D's.

SECRET #45—IT IS ACTUALLY TWO BEAUTY CONTESTS—ONE FOR COMPANIES AND ONE FOR PROSPECTS!

Of all the recruiting techniques we have discussed, this one is probably the most recent innovation.

In most cases a "job fair" is an event created by an outside enterprise which goes around the country putting on shows for job seekers. The organizer assembles a group of companies (national and local) who are recruiting, and places them in a hotel ballroom seated at tables lined up around the edges.

Attendees to the job fair are asked to dress up and bring a stack of resumes. Upon arrival, they are allowed wander around the room talking to employers with whom they might like to work, or they are herded like cattle from one table to the next.

On the positive side, most of the organizers do a pretty reasonable job of getting the word out about their shows. They also pick decent locations with good parking and adequate facilities.

On the not-so-positive side, you have to be aware that job fairs are generally nothing more than thinly disguised beauty contests for businesses.

The hiring companies compete to attract attention and draw the best candidates to their table (Everyone wants to be the most beautiful.).

Sometimes, name recognition alone is enough to get most of the <u>great</u> job prospects to line up in front of a booth. This leaves smaller local businesses out in the cold.

Other times, the businesses use other techniques to attract the job prospects. Even if the organizers place restrictions on the amount of decorations at each company's table, there are ways to get around those limitations. For one thing, the company can put extremely attractive people in their booths. For another, they may give away food or expensive premium items.

The companies will do everything in their power (and say they won't) to attract and to <u>maintain</u> the attention of the top candidates. If they engage a quality prospect in an hour-long conversation/interview in their booth, or offer to buy the candidate lunch <u>now</u>, they may be able to prevent the person from visiting a competitor's table.

On the other side of the beauty contest are the job seekers themselves. The process of talking to employers can be tiring. After a couple of hours, the candidate may not be as sharp or good-looking as he/she was at the beginning of the event. So what can he/she do?

One secret of job fairs is that the top job prospects will always try to talk to the "best" companies at the very beginning of the fair. They want to talk to the top companies, when they look their best, sound their best and smell their best.

Where does this tactic leave you, the small/medium sized local or regional business?

If you have deep pockets, you may have the financial muscle to compete with Target, Home Depot, Loews and others. If you are just a local store with a branch or two (or five) you may be left talking to weakest attendees who can't get close to the big guys.

Don't forget that, not only does your business have to look as appealing as the giants in the industry, but you also have to pay a significant fee for renting your booth space.

Admittedly, if the advertising has been done well, the job fair may draw large numbers of candidates. But, will there be enough of your "great" candidates to justify the expense of renting the table, giving away attention-getting premiums, and missing a full day of productive work at your store?

The answer is: In most cases, NO!

How can you tell that a job fair will be good or bad? You can't. There are simply no guarantees. My guess is that most of the job fair organizers will not give back your fees if an inadequate number of applicants show up.

So, all job fairs are just a bad gamble, right?

No, they don't have to be.

The giant job fair, organized by an out-of-state organizer, may be a bad gamble, but not every job fair has to be a roll of the dice.

Here's a great secret that most businesses never think of—you can always organize your own job fair.

In case you have a very short memory (like me), I want to remind you of the hiring co-ops we discussed in a previous secret. You can always get three or four retailers (like you) who are hiring, to share the cost of a meeting room at a local restaurant and some advertising (signs and flyers to schools and organizations) for your own small job fair.

Does this change the beauty contest atmosphere?

No, of course not!

What it does change though is the problem of your store/business being the small fish in a pond full of whales!

It also changes the mix of job seekers in the meeting room. By running your own retail job fair, you can be reassured that most of the candidates in the room are looking for retail work. In the larger job fairs, the room may be filled with engineers or nurses, or some other profession, that isn't interested in your industry.

If you decide to try the job fair technique, keep it simple. And keep it small (three or four hiring businesses). Outline a clear set of rules and procedures for participating businesses from the very beginning. Make sure you can trust the retailers and keep the competition friendly. As always, job seekers in attendance should be greeted promptly and made to feel welcome.

If you do one well, you will find that word-of-mouth spreads quickly. At your next one, more participants will show up and more stores will want to participate with you.

Secret #46—Shopping For Winners Produces Results!

You knew that, eventually, we had to get to my favorite recruiting technique. Finally, we're here!

It's the secret I call, "Shopping for Winners!"

Here are some of the advantages of actively going "shopping" for prospective employees:

FREE! FREE! FREE!—It literally costs nothing in dollars!

It minimizes interview time and narrows the field to the very best candidates.

It is pleasant, non-threatening and simple—anyone can do it well (with practice)!

You can do it alone, or you can get other managers in your store involved.

You don't even have to take time out of your normal work day to shop effectively!

Most importantly, IT WORKS!

Guess what? There are some disadvantages too (you probably guessed):

It requires practice!

It requires commitment and consistency!

To be effective, it <u>must</u> be done correctly!

It requires a good attitude and a clean spirit (What's that?)!

IT REQUIRES PATIENCE!

Here is how this secret "shopping" technique works—

The objective is to locate and talk to individuals whose work characteristics and behaviors seem to match your list of desired/required qualities.

For example, you might be looking for prospects who are friendly, outgoing, open and expressive. You probably would want them to SMILE and look presentable. On the other hand, you might <u>not</u> want them to display undesirable characteristics like smelling smoky or having too much body art.

To use this shopping technique, you would literally go where people with these qualities and characteristics might work—in department and discounts stores, in doctor's/dentist's offices, in dry cleaners, in specialty shops, in convenience stores or in supermarkets.

If you are looking for commissioned sales people you would probably need to look at furniture stores, high end clothing stores, appliance centers, or even car dealerships.

YES, these are all of the normal places where you usually shop anyway.

The difference between a recruiting shopping trip and your usual shopping trip is that you must pay close attention to the people who serve you <u>and</u> those who are serving other customers.

In most cases, we rush into stores and businesses, grabbing what's necessary, swiping the card or tossing the money on the counter and rushing out. We very seldom notice the store's employees—<u>unless</u> they make us angry.

Shopping for job prospects requires that you slow down and watch those around you—FOCUS. It also requires that you interact with people. For some (hermits and the painfully shy) this may present a challenge. It does not, however, have to be impossible.

Most people find it difficult or impossible to start a conversation with a total stranger.

In a store or business, it is easy. Just ask a question!!

Obviously, you would like for a sales associate, a clerk or any other employee to approach and greet you first, but if they don't, walk up to them and ask a question that generally requires some explanation. In other words, you want them to talk, so encourage it.

Ask "open-ended" questions. These are questions that require an answer longer than "yes" or "no." Here are some examples:

"Where is/are the _____?"

> I would like the person to physically show me, rather than to just point.

Or . . .

"Can you tell me the difference between _____ and _____?"

> This is a test of product knowledge and his/her willingness to help.

If the person is a clerk at a counter, you could say:

"You look like you are having a great time! Have you been doing this for long?"

Or . . .

"Thanks for smiling at me! You must really enjoy your job!"

Many times a simple question or statement is all that the person needs to start talking about themselves.

—WARNING—

In this recruiting technique, attitude is everything! You must have the proper mind set (I call it the "clean spirit.") from the start. Not everybody is a prospective employee in your store, but everybody is a prospective customer for your store! Treat people with respect and kindness!

When you start asking questions, you <u>must</u> have an honest and sincere desire to know about the person with whom you are speaking (the "clean spirit"). If you are a fake, they will know! If you don't really care, don't bother going through this process.

Here are some secrets to mastering this technique. When questioning a person—

>Shut up after you ask! You <u>never</u> learn anything when you are talking!

><u>Actively</u> listen to their answers. Pay attention!

>Don't be distracted by things happening around you or by your own mental noise.

>Make and maintain eye contact during the entire encounter.

>Don't interrupt them!!

<u>I am not psychic!</u>

But, at this moment, I know exactly what you are thinking!

You are thinking—

"He wants me to STEAL someone else's employees!!"

"I can't do this!! It will ruin my reputation with other store managers! I will ruin my reputation in town! Every store

manager in town will be coming in my store to openly steal my employees!!"

"This looks bad!!"

Am I right, or am I right?

The truth is <u>you</u> are wrong! You have jumped to a logical conclusion, but it was completely incorrect.

You are not shopping for the person who you are talking to! You are shopping for the people they know!

This is the most important part of the "clean spirit" attitude. You <u>can</u> <u>not</u> succeed at this "shopping" technique if you are thinking that you want to lure the employee (with whom you are speaking) away to work at your store.

Although some people may be initially flattered that you have chosen them as prospects, they will also have automatic reservations. Our society teaches that the entire process of luring employees away from one employer to work for another is unethical and sleazy. It looks like you are trying to <u>steal</u>. No one wants to work for a thief.

Ok, if I am not suggesting theft, what is shopping all about?

Let's go back to the truism I mentioned in our earlier secrets.

"Birds of a feather flock together."

Do you believe it?

I <u>do</u>—One Hundred and Ten Percent!!

People hang out with and befriend people who are like them!

You will <u>NEVER</u> find a person who is happy, outgoing, hardworking, loyal and trustworthy hanging out with depressed, lazy, anti-social thieves.

Good people are friends with good people! PERIOD! If I find a "good" person who hangs out with the dregs of society, I have misjudged that person! They are not really "good." They are a fake.

This is the foundation of the "shopping" concept.

The secret (and magic) message is,

"I am not after <u>you</u>! I assume you are happy and satisfied with your job. I would like to talk to your friends and acquaintances—those who might be looking for a great place to work."

(This is the paraphrased message. I don't say these exact words to the employee.)

If you buy into this concept, believe it and think it, you have a "clean spirit." You will have some outstanding results.

After you have asked an employee a few questions, they will either be a good prospect or a bad one. If they are bad, thank them for their "help" and walk away.

If they look like the kind of person you are searching for. Simply end your conversation with this statement or something close. And watch the magic happen!

"You have been a great help! Thanks!

You know, I have found that friendly, helpful, knowledgeable people, like you, <u>tend</u> to be friends with others who are friendly, helpful, and knowledgeable.

I am the manager of the XYZ Store here in town. (Give the person your card.) If any of your friends or acquaintances are looking for a job in a fun, positive environment, I would love to talk to them.

Have them give me a call, personally, and tell me that you referred them. I will give them special consideration.

Thanks again."

You will note that we have done several important things in this process. We . . .

— complimented the person with whom we spoke.
— implied that their friends are as good as they are.
— made it clear who we are.
— made it clear that we are not attempting to proselyte (trying to recruit them).
— gave a commitment that we would provide "special consideration."
— did <u>not</u> ask for any commitment from them.
— ended the conversation on a high note—no other remarks are necessary.

130

You can use your own words, but they should be close to mine (they are <u>proven</u> to work). You have to BELIEVE in what you are saying; and practice saying it. Soon it will sound natural and honest.

Practice speaking at your normal pace. Speak clearly. If necessary, have someone practice with you to make sure you sound right.

There is one final point to make about transparency.

I was born on a Tuesday, but it wasn't <u>last</u> Tuesday! I am not naïve or stupid!

I <u>know</u> that there are people who are accomplished actors (or con-artists, or both).

I am neither. I am like most other people. My intentions are always apparent by my words, my facial expressions and my body language. There is an excellent chance you are like me.

You must start out with the right attitude, or you will not be successful at having good people send their friends to talk to you. You are really looking for friends and acquaintances, <u>not</u> the people you are talking to!!

Don't try to fake the process. Believe in it or don't use it at all!!

If you use this technique properly, you will occasionally find that you are talking to good people who are unhappy or insecure in their current jobs.

Don't try to have an extended conversation with them about changing jobs while they are on someone else's time clock.

Simply reconfirm that your original intention was not to recruit them away from their current employer and ask them to give you a call or drop-by if they would like to talk.

In truth, the "shopping for winners" technique is really a modified referral system. Instead of seeking referrals from people you know, you are asking for them from people you would like to know.

If it is done exactly as I explained it above, it <u>will</u> be successful. You will be amazed at the results, BUT . . .

It will probably take some time. Be patient. Talk to as many people as possible, but don't settle for second-rate or "OK" prospects. Look for the people who seem to have all, or most, of your desired qualities in an employee.

Try walking through stores that you might not otherwise enter. If you normally shop at a store in a strip center, go into other stores in the center just to observe the employees. If you go into a department store, walk through several departments on your way out. Varying your routines slightly will not take much time, but it will help you encounter different employees on different shifts.

Perhaps most importantly, if you decide to shop for prospects, do it consistently. Make it part of your overall "Recruiting Plan."

Shopping for great prospects regularly will build your confidence and provide a more consistent stream of talented referrals for you to choose from. Shopping that is done occasionally, or on a hit-or-miss basis, relies on "dumb luck" to find good candidates.

Secret #47—Planning Isn't The Same As Having A Plan!

Thus far, we have discussed over forty-five secrets to successful retail recruiting.

Anyone who stops reading here can enjoy <u>partial</u> success simply by using a few new recruiting techniques that actually work.

This book, however, wasn't really written with <u>partial</u> success in mind. Why bother with part of something, when you can have it all, simply by creating and committing to a plan.

A solid recruiting plan ties all of the separate activities of recruiting together into a clear, unified strategy for accomplishing the ultimate goal.

Before we discuss the elements of a good recruiting plan, we need to talk about a few basics.

"Planning" to do something is <u>never</u> as good as having a "plan" to do it.

Most people don't understand this fine point.

The term, "planning," sometimes refers to the process of creating a plan, but people also say that they are planning to do something without ever developing an actual plan for its accomplishment.

Here is an example that might help—

Planning to take a vacation generally means that a person has thought about taking a vacation, but he/she probably hasn't decided on the little details like: where to go, when to go, or even how to get there. Most of the time, planning to do something is the equivalent of hoping, wishing or dreaming. There is no commitment to the completion of the project.

On the other hand, having a vacation plan implies that a person has made a solid commitment to take action and that he/she has decided on many, if not all, of the details of the trip.

Every store manager is "planning" to recruit new associates in the future, when there is an opening in his/her store.

Normally, "planning" turns into a "plan" only when a vacancy occurs. At that point, a "plan" for locating new talent is implemented.

A plan, by definition, is an outline that states who will do something, what they will do, how they will do it, when and where it will be done. A plan is not a goal. It is, however, a clear roadmap leading to the accomplishment of a goal.

Plans, like roadmaps, help the goal setter to stay on track. They minimize distractions and prevent unplanned side trips which can cost money and time.

If a real recruiting plan doesn't exist at the time of a vacancy, the store manager will generally turn to something called the "default" recruiting plan.

The default plan isn't really designed or thought out. It just happens. It relies heavily on "dumb luck."

Just a reminder: most successful managers do not consider "luck" to be an important part of their recruiting plans.

The default/dumb luck recruiting plan has two distinct elements:

— It uses recruiting techniques which have <u>always</u> been used (Status Quo). Why? *"That is just the way we do it. That is the way it has always been done."* . . . and there really isn't time to create a solid recruiting plan when an opening has got to be filled by next week!

It doesn't really matter if the recruiting systems don't work anymore, or if they <u>ever</u> worked! The plan is the plan!!

— It also requires a strong victim's mentality with a light sprinkling of laziness. The manager just accepts what has always been done without question and with very, very, very low expectations.

Here is how the default recruiting plan normally takes shape:

The store manager (any kind of retailer will do) thinks—

"I have two openings on the sales floor. I am going to try to attract as many <u>applications/resumes</u> as possible. Hopefully, out of a tall stack of paper (or a hundred e-mails), I can find a couple of good prospects."

"To draw interest, I will place a help-wanted ad in the employment section of the local newspaper for Friday, Saturday and Sunday (special package rates). I'll run the ads as long as necessary to get the applications (sometimes it takes weeks)."

"I will also place signs in the front window of the store and out by the street announcing that we are "NOW HIRING."

"After that I will just sit back and wait for the applications to come drifting in."

Here is the justification that occurs once the default plan has been implemented:

"I have done <u>everything</u> possible to find new employees!" or . . .
"I have done <u>everything</u> I am expected to do!" or . . .
"I have done everything I have time to do!"

I have heard these statements, or minor variations, at least a million times! Maybe you have even said them yourself. The only problem is that they are not true!

Managers who say these things haven't done everything possible or everything they are supposed to do or even everything they have time to do. They have done the <u>minimum</u>; those things that <u>had</u> to be done and nothing more.

Default recruiting plans aren't plans at all! They are cop-out's. They are systems which evade commitment and avoid a real recruiting plan.

Secret #48—They All Have A Plan!

A recruiting plan defines how, not if, the recruiting process will occur. It creates clarity and confidence. It helps the manager/owner to stay on track and to build a sales team that lives up to his/her expectations.

All the <u>great</u> managers have a recruiting plan—even when their floors and their stores are full of "good" associates.

Building a plan <u>is</u> possible, even if setting goals is foreign to you. It really isn't complicated. In fact, the more complicated the recruiting plan becomes, the less chance it will be followed.

The following principles are the basis for building a solid, usable recruiting plan. You will recognize several of them from previous secrets. Some are new to our discussion.

People are important to your business!

Yes, location, advertising, products and prices are important, too! But . . .

<u>Great</u> employees make <u>great</u> customer service possible!

Without great customer service a small/medium-sized business just can't compete!

Finding <u>great</u> prospects to become <u>great</u> employees can not be done as a project!

It can't be done sporadically, occasionally or just in an emergency.

Recruiting great prospects is a <u>daily</u> responsibility of every retail manager!

Effective recruiting requires a real plan!

A plan always saves time, energy and money!

SECRET #49—THE HUNT NEVER ENDS!

Yes, I said recruiting is a <u>daily</u> management responsibility!

Default recruiting has evolved directly from the <u>myth</u> that recruiting is a project.

In this faulty thought-process—a recruiting project is begun when a need arises and completed when a vacancy is filled. Between vacancies, no applications are accepted and prospects are turned away without any consideration.

This is illogical and destructive to your business!

Very few, if any, retailers can boast that their associate team is totally filled with <u>great</u> employees. There are "weak links" in almost every organization.

If you are that extraordinary manager/owner who enjoys a <u>perfect</u> associate team, you <u>might</u> be justified in discontinuing your recruiting efforts, but <u>only</u> if you are certain that you will have no turn-over.

For the rest of the world, there are always employees who are not performing well or are planning to leave.

Here is another perspective on recruiting as a project.

Will the best talent <u>always</u> be available when your store really needs them (when a vacancy occurs)? Probably not. Does it make sense to turn away or ignore great prospects because there is no current recruiting project on which you are working? Definitely not!

The quest to build a great team <u>never</u> really ends. An important secret to recruiting success is to <u>always</u> be on the hunt for great talent. If a great prospect is found and no opening currently exists, then the weakest employee can be replaced or a new position can be created. Talent should never be ignored!

Instead of being a project, recruiting must be a part of the normal daily management routine and to keep it on track, it should follow a plan.

<u>If</u> you are okay with these concepts, you are going to find the rest of the planning process to be easy.

<u>If</u> you are <u>not</u> okay with these concepts, just try to suspend your skepticism for a few moments and I will try to win you over with logic.

SECRET #50—A RECRUITING PLAN IS LIKE A STOOL!

The whole purpose of your recruiting plan is to locate the right type of prospects and bring them into your store for an interview.

Every good plan is like a three-legged stool. In order to function as designed, it <u>must</u> have three supporting elements—

Goals

Technique

Action

If any one of the supports is missing, the plan will not stand.

One reason for using the stool analogy involves simplicity.

As I mentioned before, the plan <u>must</u> be simple. The more complex the plan, the less likely it will be followed.

SECRET #51—NOT EVERYONE HAS "GOALS!"

The first leg of a recruiting plan involves the creation of GOALS.

Now, you may be thinking—

"Oh, GOALS, I have goals! Everyone has goals!"

Although you may have some real goals, don't assume everyone does!

Almost everyone has wishes, dreams and hopes, but most people do not have goals!

Take a moment to compare your "goals" to the following definitions. You may be surprised.

First, there are wishes, hopes, and dreams, which we will lump into one category, **Dreams**. These are visions (winning the lottery, going into business for yourself, finding your soul mate, losing 150 pounds, etc.) that you would like to accomplish, but, for some reason, you never do.

Second, there are **Quotas**. Almost everyone is familiar with these. If you work for a large company, you may have been told that they are the same as "Goals." This is a common misconception and another lie. Quotas are someone else's objective for you—someone else's goals. In most cases, they represent a <u>minimum</u> expected production standard for your position in the company.

Finally there are ***Goals***. In summary, they can best be described as realistic, reachable, personal objectives which you strive to accomplish. They meet <u>all</u> of the following criteria.

They are:

<u>Personal</u>—created by you, for you.
> Dreams are, too.
> Quotas are created by someone else, for them, <u>not</u> for you!

<u>Clear</u>, <u>precise</u> and <u>specific</u>. They remain clear over long or short periods of time.
> Dreams are fuzzy feelings that fade over time.
> Quotas are clear over relatively limited periods of time (months or a year)

<u>Passionate</u>, and <u>exciting</u>! They evoke very strong, positive feelings of commitment!
> Dreams evoke good, happy, warm feelings.
> Quotas generally evoke unpleasant feelings (dread) or no feelings at all.

<u>Realistic</u> and <u>attainable</u>, but cause the setter to strain for their accomplishment.
> Dreams are generally unrealistic—pleasant to think about, but unattainable.
> Quotas can range from automatically attainable (no challenge) to <u>impossible</u>.

<u>Written</u> and constantly <u>visible</u> by only <u>you</u>!

> Dreams are seldom, if ever, written—except in the pink diary under your bed.

> Quotas are always written by someone else and visible a wide variety of people.

<u>Measurable</u> and <u>Trackable</u>—progress can be measured in increments.

> Dreams are like clouds—progress toward a dream is too indistinct to measure.

> Quotas are generally very trackable (Reach them or else!).

Goals give your life direction. They are your personal destination and the plan is your map get there.

In a work environment, goals minimize the effect of distractions. They add consistency to your days and build enthusiasm for your work. They pull you out of a "blue funk" (depression) and shorten the periods of frustration we all go through.

Perhaps most importantly, the accomplishment of your goals builds self esteem and self confidence. SETTING AND REACHING PERSONAL GOALS MAKES YOU HAPPY!!!

Dreams, on the other hand, offer no support to your life whatsoever. They fill empty time with non-existent accomplishments and leave your actual life destination up to dumb luck.

Quotas are a necessary evil in some work environments, but should be seen for what they are—someone else's goals for you.

Okay, so what's the bottom line? Is this long explanation really necessary?

In a word, YES!

Part of the reason you have read this far is that greatness resides somewhere within you. You want to succeed in your business and, someplace deep inside you, you believe it is possible. Goals are like magnets, pulling you toward the accomplishments of which you know you are capable.

Always remember—

No Goals, No Greatness.

No Process (Plan), No Goals

—Only dreams.

SECRET #52—GOAL SETTING SHOULDN'T TAKE LONG!

It is time to create your recruiting goal.

I know what you have been taught.

"The goal-making process is time-consuming and mind-numbing. After several days of pondering and weighing my options, I will be forced to choose goals that make everyone happy, but me. I will feel pressured and stressed by the process, and, in all likelihood, embarrassed by the outcome."

"As soon as I finish the grueling process of making the goals, because it was so painful, I will hide the results in a stack (if I actually wrote them down) and not look at them until next year, if then (my own version of a time capsule)."

Secret—that's <u>not</u> the way this works.

Allow <u>10 minutes</u>—no longer—for the entire goal-setting process!

As you work through the process, do the following:

#1—Just think about a "RECRUITING" goal. Don't try to set goals for any other project during this session.

#2—These will be <u>your</u> goals, not mine or anyone else's. Focus on serving the needs of your customers. They will ultimately determine the level of your success.

#3—KEEP IT SIMPLE!! You will need a piece of paper and a pen. You <u>don't</u> need any fancy or expensive goal-making systems—no leather bound trackers, no complex software systems, no magic techniques developed by a famous CEO.

#4—Find a CLEAN area on which to work! If you are one of those people who can't remember the color of the top of their desk, or if you don't really have a desk, you can always do this at home or down the street at the café/donut shop (I will have a chocolate glazed, please.).

#5—ELIMINATE interruptions and distractions. You'll probably notice that I didn't say "avoid" or "minimize." I know you are vital to the operation of your store, but I also know that, for ten minutes, everyone can get by without bugging you.

#6—You receive no bonus credit for neatness! Just get the project done.

#7—Stop messing around! Do it now! No procrastination! No endless preparation!

Now, take your piece of paper and your pen.

At the top of the paper, write today's date.

Next, write down the following (you will need this information later):

— The number of employees you need to be <u>fully staffed</u> (based on current sales),

— The number you need just to <u>cover</u> (minimum number to run the store),

— The number of associates who actually work for your store today,

— The number of your <u>weak</u> associates who have "acceptable" skills,

— The number of your <u>weak</u> associates who have "unacceptable" skills.

Before we go on, here is a quick thought about being "fully staffed"—

At first blush, it seems logical to work toward a "full" sales floor/office/backroom (all openings filled) by today's standards.

In reality, "fully staffed," as you define it today, may not be necessary or desirable.

Normally it takes fewer competent, reliable, talented sales associates to run a store than if the store was fully staffed with incompetent, unreliable, untalented sales people.

A store with great sales associates will undoubtedly save personnel costs, because fewer people are needed to provide great service! Oh, and by the way, total sales will also increase.

It's just something to keep in mind.

You get to decide what "weak," "acceptable" and "unacceptable" mean, using your desired characteristics (R's & D's) list.

Just write down whatever numbers come to your mind. In most cases, the first estimates are the best. Don't rationalize. Try to avoid emotions. This will be of great importance later.

You might find yourself saying,

"All of my people are 'great!'"

Or

"I don't have any weak or terrible sales people,"

You are either blessed beyond measure, or you are living in a happy fairytale land with lollipops and candy canes.

If you don't have an immediate feeling about which of your people are "weak," you may be out of touch with your sales floor. There is no magic formula for determining this information. If you don't know, get out of your office and spend some time watching your people work.

I realize that these are tough questions. They require you to be a tough manager but no one ever said being successful was easy.

Now, here's your next step.

Subtract the total number of weak associates (with and without acceptable skills) from the total number of associates currently employed in your store. The remainder is your "good" or "great" employees.

"Good" or "great" means that they meet, or exceed, <u>your</u> standards for customer service, friendliness, honesty, enthusiasm, appearance, professionalism, product knowledge and sales ability.

If the number is greater than zero, congratulations, you have some quality associates!

If the number is zero, we obviously have some work to do.

If the number is less than zero, you screwed up on the math.

SECRET #53—THERE ARE TWO TYPES OF JOB OPENINGS ON YOUR FLOOR!

Secret—Two types of job openings that exist in your store at any moment.

First, there are the <u>critical openings</u>.

These are the openings that <u>must</u> be filled ASAP. If you are so short of personnel that your associates are forced to work overtime to cover the schedule, you definitely have some critical openings.

Another critical opening is the sales associate with unacceptable skills who is currently employed by your store. It is important that you terminate them and replace them as soon as you can.

In most cases, (unless you are severely understaffed) the negative, poorly skilled, unmotivated or uncaring sales people do much more damage to customer service (and SALES) than having no sales person at all!

On the surface it may seem like I am saying that terminating bad sales people (even with no immediate replacement) might <u>improve</u> customer service/sales in your store.

YES, that is exactly what I am saying!

**Farm Wisdom
From Your Humble Author**

One rotten apple will spoil the barrel

-including new apples added to the barrel in the future.

Get rid of the rotten apples!

Second, there are the "casual" openings.

These job openings exist, but it isn't critical that they be filled right away.

— Perhaps the floor is covered, but some customers aren't receiving prompt attention and the store could use more help. In this case, it might be nice to find an additional associate or two.

— Maybe you know an employee who will be leaving in the near future (depending on what "near" means).

— If a weak employee does not have <u>enough</u> of the D's (desired characteristics) to be considered a good associate, he/she is a candidate for "casual" replacement.

Yes, I just suggested that regardless of how "nice" or loyal employees have been, they should be <u>replaced</u> if they have can't be classified as good or great!

There are two distinct advantages to this tactic.

First, the knowledge that you are recruiting new sales people and replacing the poor ones could have a strong, positive motivational effect on all remaining sales people on your floor. Top producers will be encouraged when they see better talent replace no talent. Poor producers will be encouraged to perform better for fear of being replaced.

It is actually de-motivating for your good sales associates to believe that poor performers might never be eliminated. Also, the weak associates may become even more complacent, thinking that they probably won't be fired or replaced regardless of their performance.

Second, sales people with poor skills or poor attitudes have a tendency to bring down the entire team (see Farm Wisdom above). If you hire a new promising sales person and throw them into a team with very weak producers, they may lose some or all of their motivation to perform at top levels.

It goes without saying that your goal will be to fill the critical openings first, and quickly. Then you can start to fill your "casual" openings.

This brings us to a very important point in the goal-making process.

It is tempting to create GIANT goals—especially if you are aggressive, or you have a disaster in progress.

Really big goals may be thrilling in the beginning, but they can also lead to an unnecessary chain of events. They can add incredible amounts of stress to an already difficult situation. As the recruiting progress slows and stalls due to unrealistic expectations, the goal-setter's efforts may become desperate and inconsistent. If the sky-high goals aren't reached in the expected timeframe, the manager can become frustrated and lose self esteem.

STOP! Don't let this happen to you!

No matter how bad the problem is, keep your goals reasonable and reachable. Goal setting works best when it is approached logically, consistently and with controlled emotions (I told you this would be important later).

Finally, it's time to set your recruiting goal. It's based on the five numbers you have calculated up to this point.

SECRET #54—RECRUITING GOAL = INTERVIEWS, NOT HIRES!

Your "recruiting goal" is the number of good or great candidates you would like to interview during a period of time (I suggest a week)—not hire, just interview.

Depending on your critical needs, your number should probably be between 2 and 5. If you have a personnel disaster on your hands, you can certainly start out with a goal to have as many as necessary.

Let me guess your response, *"What? If I have only two to five interviews per week, I will never find anyone to hire!!"*

In the past, you probably interviewed anyone who could walk and breath (hopefully at the same time) hoping to find anyone decent (translation—barely acceptable) to hire.

That is a dumb strategy. Sorry if that hurt someone's feelings.

Earlier in this book, you created a profile of a "great" associate prospect (when you made the list of R's and D's). Now, you are deciding how many of those "great" candidates you want to see each and every week. It obviously takes a lot more time and effort to see 5 prospects per week than it does to see two.

If you are going to implement a recruiting plan that becomes part of your daily managerial activities, you can't afford to waste time interviewing anyone who doesn't meet your standards for "good" or "great."

The real question here is, if you were interviewing good or great candidates, how many interviews would you need to conduct in order to find one person you would hire? It might be tempting to say one, but you need to allow for a few bad apples in your prospecting barrel and a few great people who decide not to work for you.

Remember this goal is <u>yours</u>, not mine, give it some serious thought.

The great thing about your recruiting goal is that it is not written in stone (just on paper). Goals can be adjusted and tested and adjusted again. The important thing is to be realistic and reasonable. Choose a number of interviews that you think you can conduct comfortably, based on your schedule and your needs.

Now write down your recruiting goal—the number of good or great prospects you want to locate and interview each week.

SECRET #55—TEST YOUR PROPECTING TECHNIQUE(S)!

In order to reach your recruiting goal you must next select the method(s) you will use to find the best possible candidates. This is the second leg of the stool.

Good News! We have already listed over twenty different recruiting techniques, systems and processes for locating great candidates. You may have come up with some others I left out.

Select one or two recruiting systems that you like and believe will work for you; in your city. Don't choose more than two. I will explain why shortly.

How do you know which one's will work best?

You don't. You do know which ones generally don't work!

There are, of course, no guarantees. You should select a recruiting technique(s) that fits your budget and your personality first, and your community second (large city, small town, etc.).

Once you have made your selection(s), write it/them down on your goal page.

Keep in mind that very few of the recruiting techniques we have discussed will produce prospects immediately. Some will take a week. Some will take longer to become fully operational and begin yielding candidates to work in your store.

Once a recruiting technique is fully operational, test it for three to six weeks. During the test period, keep careful records of how many good/great prospects were generated and how many bad prospects were generated.

If you don't already know, be sure to ask every candidate how he/she found out that you were looking for quality talent. This will tell you which prospecting technique produced the results.

Please don't get wrapped up in the "careful records" terminology. Remember, you have to keep it simple! Use marks on your goal page to indicate how many prospects (good, great or bad, three columns) each technique brings in.

If any recruiting technique produces large numbers of quality candidates, it goes without saying, keep using it. If, on the other hand, the recruiting technique generates poor results—no good/great candidates or too many weak candidates—DUMP IT and try something else!

SECRET #56—MAKE IT A HABIT!

Schedule the same time <u>each</u> <u>day</u> for recruiting—normally fifteen to thirty minutes. Select activities which support your chosen recruiting techniques and move you toward the accomplishment of your goals—making phone calls, visiting centers of influence, "shopping" in local stores/restaurants, putting together recruiting materials or other recruiting activities.

The objective is to create a good habit. Conventional wisdom (whatever that is) says that repeating a task thirteen to fifteen times creates a habit which will become a permanent part of your daily activities. I say, "You can't do enough repetitions! Keep doing it! If you stop pumping, the well stops producing water!"

Let's summarize what we covered thus far in this discussion of the second leg:

- Pick a recruiting technique (or two)—write it down.
- Test it/them for three to five weeks.
- Record the results generated by each technique—good, great and bad.
- Schedule recruiting efforts for the same time each day—fifteen to thirty minutes.

Finally, place/hang/post your recruiting goals page in a place where you can see it and others can't.

You may have heard from "experts" who say that your goals and your plans should be shared with others,

"This motivates you to stay on track. The potential embarrassment of not reaching your goals, with everybody watching, will keep you going."

I say, don't show your goals or your plans to <u>anyone</u> (except maybe a boss or a significant other). This is <u>your</u> project. Your employees may feel threatened by your efforts, your colleagues may be jealous, your friends probably won't understand anyway. Just get to work and let everyone marvel at your results!

SECRET #57—CONSISTENT EFFORT CREATES REALITY!

For years, authors have devoted entire books to the subject of taking action—the third leg of our recruiting plan "stool." Consistent with our mission (keep it short and direct), I will devote entire sentences (and probably a few sentence fragments) to the subject.

We will be talking about, not just taking action, but taking the _right_ action.

Understanding the difference is critical to your ultimate success!

Let's start with a question,

Have you ever known people who are like this?

They start projects with unbridled enthusiasm, excitement and passion. They have only the very best of intentions! They tell everyone what they are doing.

Within a few days or a couple of weeks, their project begins to drag and some (or all) of the enthusiasm fades.

Within a few more days, their project is no longer mentioned. Without enthusiastic support, the great project slips away into oblivion, never to be heard from again.

Most of us have seen it happen dozens, maybe hundreds, of times (often involving weight loss goals). I have personally done it to myself more times than I am willing to admit. It is an agonizingly painful form of self torture.

And yet, many of us will wait a while and do it all over again.

Our society places great value on speed. Moving fast isn't limited to cars and airplanes. We expect our personal and business projects to move fast, too.

Consider the weight loss example mentioned above:

We need to lose a few dozen pounds which have been lovingly packed-on over the last several years. We want to start fast, work without exertion and see the pounds melt away in days. We expect that any obstacles we encounter will be swept away like leaves blown in the tailwind of a speeding Ferrari.

The TV commercials say that years of blubber will be reduced to rock-hard abs, ready for the beach, in only six weeks, or three weeks, or ten days!

It must be true or they couldn't say it on television! Right?

No, of course not!

Here is the <u>truth</u> about goals and the time it takes to achieve them.

Reaching a goal (<u>any</u> goal) requires the application of <u>consistent</u> effort over a "reasonable" period of time, as well as, <u>unwavering</u> commitment to the process AND the goal.

The secret here is that <u>consistent</u> effort creates reality!!

- Consistent eating and lack of exercise creates obesity.
- Consistent exercise and good diet creates rock hard abs and a small waist.
- Consistent worry creates ulcers.
- Consistent recruiting creates a GREAT team of retail sales associates!

Most people would agree with these statements, but very few would agree on the meaning of the term "reasonable."

Today, our "reasonable" is shaped by the unrealistic expectations which have been formed by television and the Internet, demanding bosses/owners, and our own anxious insecurities.

For our recruiting purposes, "reasonable" is going to be defined by your market, your store and your needs. It is also going to be affected by the number of people you know and your ability to build strong relationships.

Be patient. Start <u>today</u>, during your scheduled recruiting time.

Don't begin with a blast of energy and enthusiasm that will be totally expended within a few days! Develop a <u>steady</u> pace—one that can be maintained for a long time!

You can't force things happen on your time schedule, but you can allow them to happen when the time is right. Do everything possible to take personal anxieties and business pressures out of the mix.

It's inevitable. After reading this entire book some people are still going say:

"This is silly or stupid! I don't care what proof you have to the contrary, these techniques won't work. My town, my store, my situation is totally different!"

Or

"I just don't have the time to recruit every day! My day is full! I am just too busy!"

Or

"Recruiting is <u>impossible</u> in my town! There are no great prospects here! No one wants to work anymore!"

All I can say about that way of thinking is . . .

THANKS!

I <u>really</u> do appreciate people who say these things. I am also grateful for their willingness to read this far and consider the concepts presented here.

I am sorry, however, that they have chosen to be victims.

Although they may prefer to be called "critical thinkers" (they are also known as "cynics"), these people exhibit all of the classic qualities of a victim of society—helpless and hopeless.

They believe, with every fiber of their being, that they are prevented, by harsh circumstance (or paralyzing fear), from <u>ever</u> realizing greatness. They see themselves as blocked at every turn and bound by the "way things are."

I am not going to say that I understand this mentality, but I do appreciate it!

Victims (cynics) keep the paths to greatness clear. They see roadblocks that prevent them from ever getting out into the traffic traveling to the top of the retail mountain. Their attitude keeps them out of the way of those brave, daring souls who are out to accomplish the "impossible."

The secrets presented in this book aren't radical or mysterious. None of them are so outlandish that they defy logic or reason. All of them do, however, require an acceptance that the Status Quo is no longer working in retail recruiting and needs to be changed!

The victims or the cynics will always say, "It can't be done!"

The future winners will always say, "Let's give it a try. What do we have to lose?"

Now, be honest!

Does it sound like I'm suggesting this is a mental game? Am I saying that a secret to your future recruiting success is dependent to a large extent on YOUR MENTAL ATTITUDE?

Good observation!

I'm letting you know, that going through the motions, playing the part, will never be enough to create ultimate success!

Great retail managers <u>think</u> like great retail managers. That is to say, they believe in their mission and they understand that some of the greatest obstacles they will ever face are in their own minds. They refuse to accept failure as an option.

I know you have heard these revelations before. I also know that it sounds all preachy. But, I have actually observed the truth and I owe it to you to tell you <u>all</u> of the secrets to recruiting, and, for that matter, management success.

Whether you decide to use this secret is ultimately your choice. You may have the will-power to change a few of your daily activities, but do you have the strength to change <u>you</u>?

Congratulations! If you implemented the secrets revealed above, you have just finished building a solid recruiting plan!

Secret #59—The Unbeatable Advantage Of Being Small!

We have talked about a total of 58 secrets so far.

There is only <u>ONE</u> <u>more</u> to go!

Let's take a minute and look at the big picture.

As we discussed earlier, the giants (the Mega stores) and the Internet are quick to tout their "unbeatable" advantages over the little guys (small/medium sized, local retailers)—LAPP. They are always careful to ignore Customer Service of course, because they provide so little of it.

This short-coming creates a tremendous opportunity for smaller retailers to flourish.

The only real challenge is PEOPLE!

Since employees/associates remain the <u>only</u> source of good customer service. The ability of any store to provide a high level of support for shoppers is dependent on recruiting <u>enough</u> of the right people to serve their customers' needs.

<u>Top</u> retail managers and owners:

- Take action quickly—no hesitation, no procrastination
- Create a profile of the R's & D's of a <u>great</u> sales associate.

- Set realistic, attainable recruiting goals.
- Develop a written plan for reaching those goals.
- Set aside time <u>every</u> day to work their recruiting plan.
- Test recruiting techniques and continue to use those that <u>work</u>.
- Have a <u>great</u> mental attitude

Thus far, in our discussion, only one piece of the puzzle has been left out—control.

Every retail professional (whether owner or manager) has <u>some</u> control over their business activities—how, when, where they do business (even the Mega-Store managers).

Every retail professional also has some limitations which are placed on their control.

At this point, some owners may doubt the truth of this statement. They may be thinking that they have <u>total</u> control of their business—no limitations.

Let's consider that perspective—

Even if they own their business outright (no inventory or cash receivable loans), owners have personal limitations on the amount of money they can spend (no bottomless pits of cash here) and on the amount of time they can devote to the store. They may have families and they have to sleep. Right?

They are also limited by laws, regulations and ethics which constrain <u>every</u> business.

So even if you are an owner, you have some limitations on the way you conduct business. There is no total control.

This is good news and bad news.

The bad news is that we have any limitations at all (Yes, I am a shameless Capitalist!).

The good news is that the limitations vary widely. The small to medium sized business owners and managers have much greater control and fewer limitations than the manager in a Mega-store.

This leads us to a BIG secret, so don't tell anyone.

The giant retailers have grown so large, and are so totally invested in LAPP (location, advertising, product selection & low, low prices), that they are no longer capable of providing good customer service, at all!

Super store general managers can't control the quality or the quantity of the associates in their stores because the low prices and giant buildings require tight limits on personnel costs (including recruiting costs) and create long chains of command. They may want to go out and prospect for great employees (Yeah, right!), but they have twenty assistants to oversee and the assistants are only interested in keeping the GM off their backs!

The big-boys in the ivory tower might want good customer service at the individual store level, but the message received at the bottom is "hire whoever you can find to work for minimum wages (with no benefits) and, occasionally, remind them to be nice to customers."

If you are a small or medium sized business owner or manager, this is your unbeatable advantage over the retail giants.

You can't control everything about your business, but you can control customer service and the people who provide it!

You can recruit the BEST people in your market and you can provide what your customers want and need—help, support, SERVICE provided by friendly, knowledgeable, positive sales associates!

People will always go to the retail giants to get some cheap items, but where will they go for personal assistance. The small/medium sized retailer is their only hope!

> **Always Remember—**
>
> Great customers <u>do</u> <u>not</u> create great employees but . . .
>
> Great employees <u>do</u> create great customers (happy, satisfied, <u>repeat</u> customers)!

Still not convinced?

It's okay. I tried my best.

You can continue recruiting and doing business like you always have.

If it doesn't work out, the Super Store down the block is probably hiring!

"Welcome to WalMart!"

By the way, I still don't know where to find the Super Glue and the brown rice!

The End

ABOUT THE AUTHOR

"Who Is This Guy, Anyway?"

Hi, I am James W. Cole, otherwise known as "your humble author." My friends just call me "Jim."

I am a salesman, a sales manager, a sales trainer and, of course, a sales recruiter. Over the last thirty years or so, I have trained thousands of sales professionals and recruited several hundred.

During my career, I have worked both in retail and in direct sales. The primary difference between the two is that in direct sales people are generally responsible for locating their own new customers. In retail, the majority of sales people just wait around for customers to "magically" appear at their doorstep.

Until recently, I was the senior sales trainer for a regional furniture company.

I am currently a consultant to small and medium sized retail businesses. I help managers and owners solve sales-related challenges in their stores.

I am also a speaker and an independent trainer for retailers.

I have previously written sales training manuals and several articles in professional journals and magazines.

I live in Texas with my wife, Diane. I am an avid marathon/half-marathon runner. I have two children and four <u>beautiful</u> grandchildren (The children are pretty good looking, too!).

I enjoy working with great managers/owners and those who want to be great.

Business consultations are generally handled by phone. It keeps costs low and maximizes time investments.

If you want to talk about your retail sales challenge or if you need a speaker on sales topics, give me a call at (512) 632-9648 or send me an e-mail at <u>jwcclu@hotmail.com</u>.

Good Selling!